Soul Mates Journey To Heaven

INTRODUCTION SERIES

God's romantic love, pure love is giving your life for the one you love, with loving kindness eternally, Thomas and Ginette, miraculously brought together through grace, prayers, faith, and their love for God. "It's who you are – not what you have"

HERB KLINGELE

BALBOA.PRESS
A DIVISION OF HAY HOUSE

KJV "Scripture quotations marked KJV are from the Holy Bible, King James Version (Authorized Version). First published in 1611. Quoted from the KJV Classic Reference Bible, Copyright © 1983 by The Zondervan Corporation"

Balboa Press books may be ordered through booksellers or by contacting:

Balboa Press
A Division of Hay House
1663 Liberty Drive
Bloomington, IN 47403
www.balboapress.com
844-682-1282

Print information available on the last page.

ISBN: 978-1-9822-6472-7 (sc)
ISBN: 978-1-9822-6473-4 (e)

Balboa Press rev. date: 02/26/2021

Romance and love are ageless. Dating should be about selecting, not being selected. Do not be in love with the dream: you may compromise. Do not find somebody you can live with: find someone you cannot live without. 1 Peter 3: 7. Likewise, ye husbands, dwell with your wife according to knowledge, giving honor unto the wife, as unto the weaker vessel, and as being heirs together of the grace of life: that your prayers be not hindered. Men, if you do not honor your wife along with grace, your prayers will not be answered.

CONTENTS

DEDICATION

Herb's brother Jack and his wife Shirley, dedicated to family love, celebrating 50 years of marriage on Valentine's Day, 14 February 2021 the year of our Lord, (married 1971). Herb is proud of his brother Jack and his wife, setting an example of love endured through their trials and tribulations together.

Herb considers this most certainly, the soul's journey to heaven. Herb would like to thank his brother Jack, and God continuously is with Jack and his family, through Jesus Christ our Lord's name.

Be nice to yourself, Jack and Shirley, because you're worth it. No worry, no stress, for that is a moment of happiness you will never get back. God's gift to us is life: what we do with this life is our gift to God.

Bob "the slob" Dalton, one of Herb's best friends, Herb and Bob met one another working at the same garbage company together when Herb was 16 years old. Bob a significant contributor to the publishing of this book.

Herb would like to give thanks and appreciation for all the years they have known one another. With their loving friendship through the grace of God, these two friends find themselves, reflecting on how fortunate they are, to still be alive through their trials and tribulations, beyond miraculous.

FOREWORD

Thomas and Ginette were inspired to write this book pertaining to this love that is very romantic, sensual, and spiritual. With spiritual discernment to help other relationships, engagement, marriage, and romantic love, not for profit or prestige, proceeds donated. Their priorities to find a Christian love equally yoked spiritually that 99.9% of others do not see.

Hang on for the ride. Thomas and Ginette's love for one another will bear witness to a roller coaster at first, level out, and keep on cruising. See if you can put down this book, as this loving documentary will keep you on the edge of your seat from the first to the last sentence.

Ginette is also looking for love. Driven spiritually, she must continue to correspond with Thomas and should be putting everything in prayers.

1 John 4:1 *Beloved, do not believe every spirit but test the spirits to see whether they are from God, for many false prophets have gone out into the world.*

ACKNOWLEDGMENTS

Sacred acknowledgment: God's love only from Grace of God. Jesus Christ our Lord and Savior, went to the cross for our wretched sins, to save our precious souls. The Holy Spirit, the gift to pray (ask in faith believing), heal, and cast out evil spirits.

Ginette has been talking to her Mom (Diane) about Thomas for a while now, and she thinks he will be the right person for her. Ginette's mom also advised her daughter to love and respect him.

1 Peter 3:1. *Likewise, ye wives, be in subjection to your husbands: if any obey not the word, they also may without the word be won by the wives' conversation.*

They will see that you live holy lives and respect your husbands. Prayer produces intimacy, and you are intimate with the one you pray with. When a man prays for his wife and with his wife, they become inseparable. Without spiritual intimacy, there can be no sexual intimacy. Proverbs 31: 10. Who can find a virtuous woman? For her, the price is far above rubies.

And a loving caring mother, Ginette has let her mom see Thomas's picture and a few of the emails that Thomas has sent to Ginette.

Thomas and Ginette would like to thank everyone throughout this soul's journey experience. This phenomenal Grace from God, Thomas, and Ginette's unshakable Faith. The amazing love from God, "that has no beginning or no end." Learning how to tap into that love has brought great joy through the miracles Thomas and Ginette have experienced together.

Ginette's mom said, "respect him" "he is an honest heart, looking for a like-minded person," she encourages Ginette not to look at age, but the real moral character of trust and honesty.

Ginette's mom thinks Thomas is good-looking. Ginette's mom has insight and intuition that only a loving mother could have. Ginette's mom also believes her daughter and Thomas are looking for the same thing. 2 Corinthians 6: 14 *Do not be unequally yoked with unbelievers. For what partnership has righteousness with lawlessness? Or what fellowship has the light with darkness?*

PREFACE

In a lazy mindset, after chatting and emailing hundreds of ladies over the last four years, Thomas concluded that his soul mate was not of this earth but was awaiting his arrival in heaven. Thomas went on a Christian dating site and placed his profile as he has on many other websites.

Thomas always made it a point never to pay money going on to these websites. For quite some time, Thomas has been praying, residing his soul mate would have to be a miracle from God. God answered Thomas's prayer in such a way that merely shocked Thomas. Contacted by a gorgeous lady named Ginette, what set her apart from all the others, was the tremendous long email that she had sent, a maiden voyage, for not only Ginette, Thomas as well.

Immediately praying to God and questioning God's choice, Thomas said, "God, you have to be kidding"? With overwhelming joy, Thomas, in hopes of a miracle that had been elusive, right in front of his eyes. Ginette, this beautiful lady, and Thomas good- looking. Thomas immediately emptied his soul to Ginette, not leaving one stone unturned or one thought. Thomas tried to discourage Ginette from getting into a relationship with him in his infinite wisdom and lifelong experiences.

Ginette was steadfast in her excitement of finding a love she also had never expected and entirely accepted it from day one.

INTRODUCTION

Ginette is from Canada, gifted at speaking French and English fluently. Thomas is from the United States in the state of Arizona. These remote communications are intriguing and very romantic, as they cannot seem to separate themselves.

This manuscript is designed to answer the question and help others in a marriage, relationship, or dead and dying marriage. That can be equally developed spiritually.

Both Thomas and Ginette are looking for the same thing, and a spiritual partner is equally yoked in marriage. They are both Christians, and they devote their lives to helping others and doing God's will together. The first and only question that comes to everyone's mind is, will they enjoy lifelong compatibility with one another?

Ginette has lived alone for the last three years, and Thomas has lived alone for four years. They continue communicating online for the last 6 to 9 months daily. Their attraction for one another is magnetic and robust: through chatting online, they get to know one another reasonably well. Then there comes a time to extend the communication with telephone calls. Ginette is tired of dating men, is bored because of their immaturity and lack of understanding.

Ginette works very hard 5 to 6 days a week as a waitress in an exclusive restaurant. Every spare moment she gets, she finds herself either calling Thomas on the telephone or chatting online, deepening and strengthening their love for one another.

Ginette is planning a trip to Arizona to meet Thomas. Finally, find out about their life, trials, and tribulations together and the sensual, romantic, spiritual love they have for one another, from the Grace of God, their faith, and prayers.

Ginette finally meets Thomas at the airport, and Thomas has a friend that owns a limousine service. Without saying a word to one another, the spiritual connection was overwhelming. Everything happens for a reason, and nothing happens perchance: this romantic interlude between Thomas and Ginette is a relationship made in heaven.

The doubts dissipate rapidly. As Thomas and Ginette realize that God did not go on vacation and leave anyone in charge, thank God. John 3: 16 *"For God so loved the world, that He gave His only begotten Son, that whoever believes in Him should not perish but have eternal life."*

Romans 14: 10 –13. *Why do you pass judgment on your brother? Or you, why do you despise your brother? For we will all stand before the judgment seat of God: for it is written, "As I live, says the Lord, every knee shall bow to me, and every tongue shall confess to God."* So then each of us will give an account of himself to God.

Therefore let us not pass judgment on one another any longer, but rather decide never to put a stumbling block or hindrance in the way of a brother. Luke 6: 37. *"Judge not, and you will not be judged: condemn not, and you will not be doomed: forgive, and you will be forgiven:*

Timothy: 2:19, *Nevertheless, the foundation of God standeth sure, having this seal, The Lord knoweth them that are his. And, Let everyone that nameth the name of Christ depart from iniquity.* Thessalonians 5: 2. – *For yourselves know perfectly that the day of the Lord, so comes as a thief in the night.*

Thomas and Ginette are blessed with a beautiful smile. A smile can be an answer to a prayer for someone in need. A smile can relieve the everyday trials and tribulations others encounter by giving that smile freely to someone who needs it. We should give it away to keep it, and the smile is a simple way to mend a broken heart. A smile can relieve depression and worry for some lost soul. The majority can smile, but many do not.

All we can offer is a brilliant smile in remembrance of love and eternal love with happiness. Keep that smile on your face with an appreciation that you are blessed: God is with us every minute of every day: all you have to do is call on the Lord and pray.

FROM PREVIOUS BOOK

"Annie And The Gigolo's"

If you will notice a book in the author's arsenal, "Annie and the gigolo." In this manuscript, there is a love between Annie through an online dating service of how most couples meet. As a result, Annie falls in love with a gentleman, and this goes on and on.

Through Annie's pictures and all of her lies, deceit, and fraudulent ways, you will find, for the most part, if you're looking at the pictures. Possibly you are not looking at the picture you think you're looking at, and you tend to fall in love because of the words this fraudulent lady Annie keeps promising love sending more pictures. And behind Annie's deceitful dark lurching ways is a gigolo. This gigolo controls ladies and supposedly protect them.

However, we have found out through experience these gigolos are nothing but cowards and hide behind these ladies taking Annie's money as fast as the online sucker man who keeps providing with false promises.

John 8:44 *Ye are of your father the devil, and the lusts of your father ye will do. He was a murderer from the beginning, and abode not in the truth, because there is no truth in him. When he speaketh a lie, he speaketh of his own: for he is a liar, and the father of it.*

This goes on for quite some time between Thomas and Annie. Thomas has a suspicion because of the lies that he lets go because he has fallen in love with Annie. And she keeps dangling the carrot in front of him even though Thomas knows he is being taken advantage of with the thoughts that possibly one day they will get together and get married.

How Thomas found out was through a publishing agent from the Philippines that noticed that this lady Annie was a phony, which led Thomas to investigate. Thomas was in total disbelief. Sure enough, the more research you did, the more he found out about all the lies and he was telling him. She was on numerous dating sites and even made pornography movies and model for pornography films and shots of pictures.

And one thing Annie never did was share her life with Thomas. Thomas emptied his soul to her, and she gave nothing in return. Not even a postcard, and when Thomas found out the pictures,

Annie was not. As Thomas confronted Annie, she denied it and lied and lied and made up some big excuse and even got angry that Thomas would even insinuate such an accusation.

And then she stopped sending pictures at all. All she was interested in was using Thomas's address to have computers, and iPhone sent to Thomas, and Thomas would send them on to an address in New York City. From there, they would be mailed to Annie and her gigolo, more than likely in Africa where they could get big money for these items. Thomas noticed they were using other Social Security numbers for the purchase and delivered to Thomas's home.

Thomas lives alone in what used to be a bachelor pad, and the promises of Annie to come and live with Thomas found Thomas remodeling this house into a beautiful home. Thomas always looks at the right side of things and looks at the good stuff he has brought into his life.

Thomas now has that beautifully remodeled home he has turned his life around: as far as looking at pornography, he finds it repulsive. Andy has dove headfirst into theology and studying the Bible almost 24 hours a day, devoting his life to God and service as you will keep reading the love Thomas as for God through prayers, faith, and love for God through Jesus Christ our Lord's name in the Holy Spirit that moves throughout the earth answering prayers.

Thomas found himself praying and praying to God, saying, please, God help me find out if this girl Annie is for real or is you fraudulent and deceitful? It did not take Thomas but two days unbeknownst to him.

He sent his fiancée Annie $50 one day through PayPal and came to find out, and he did not have a PayPal account. So Annie used what she claimed to be a friend of her statement. And was the same name and a different email address, only having her last name and her first initial. Thomas thought it was on the up and up. Annie and her fiancé seem to be on the up and up until she was not contacting him, so Thomas thought he would send an email to the email account on PayPal and three other emails that Annie has.

The prayers paid off, and a miracle happened.

A different lady responded to Thomas, and she mentioned not to send any more emails to Annie because she was a fraud. Thomas was a little shocked: this lady even gave Thomas her telephone number. And her first name is Ginette.

So Thomas called her instantly when she gave him her telephone number. She sounded very charming, and if you can believe this or not, God has a strange way. Ginette's fiancé was not calling her on the telephone and was taking money from her, and she wanted to know if I would contact him on Christmas to wish him a Merry Christmas. After talking for some time, Thomas found out that Annie was with a gigolo named Mark.

Mark was Annie's Step-Father.

And it was Ginette's fiancé. It was getting confusing so hang on for this ride. It seems Ginette's fiancé Mark had taken or stolen Ginette's passport. Then he gave it to his friend Annie and somehow, the gigolo Mark had taken Annie's picture and somehow patched it onto the passport of Ginette. And then the gigolo gave the passport to Annie to use fraudulently. Without Ginette's knowledge.

Thomas and Ginette talked daily to get to know one another and find out what Annie and her gigolo Mark were doing. And only God knows their real names. It seems Annie's gigolo Mark swindled Ginette out of $8000. And love has a strange way. Ginette was madly in love with Mark even after this gigolo ripped her off and would not call her or let Ginette know where he was staying. Thomas instantly picked up on it and said, are you serious? Mark and Annie are in bed together. And Ginette, you are what I have been praying for to God. You are a miracle.

The money I sent to Annie was from Ginette's PayPal account. And Annie used Ginette's passport, which Ginette's signature, although the passport was not Ginette's picture. What a mess: it even gives me a headache writing about this. Ginette is such a sweetheart, and she has never lied to me, and she said first things, she will never lie to me. So day after day we talk on the telephone and send each other emails. Although Thomas cannot convince Ginette that her fiancé, gigolo, is taking advantage of her, she is that much in love with him.

Although Thomas continues chipping away a little at a time, Ginette finally starts to see the light. Thomas and Ginette are also Christians equally yoked spiritually. They have more in common than they ever thought they had. They are falling in love with each other. The gigolo and Annie are French-Canadian as well as Ginette. Thomas is skeptical and in a state of disbelief, thinking this is another con, and it very well could be. However, Ginette sounds so sincere and wants to meet Thomas as soon as possible in Arizona. Although because of this, coronavirus has the whole world and locked down.

As soon as they get the opportunity, they plan on coming together. Thomas let Ginette know that he will not fornicate he is a Christian and loves God, and wants to do it right this time. The Internet seems to agree. Sex outside of marriage is a sin and abomination against God.

1 Corinthians 7:2 *Nevertheless, to avoid fornication, let every man have his own wife, and let every woman have her own husband.* Romans 1:29 *Being filled with all unrighteousness, fornication, wickedness, covetousness, maliciousness: full of envy, murder, debate, deceit, malignity: whisperers.* Thomas has researched so many online dating scams, like the picture.

Annie was using (*Janessa*) this beautiful model from Brazil who 86 romance scammers are using her photos.

Thomas finally talked of her video-chatted lovely lady and said she is finished with the business, although she still does, I guess naked chatting, and whatever they call that. However, she's out of the industry of pornography. And seem to be down-to-earth and honest. After video chatting and seeing her in person finally, Thomas has found the real Annie.

Janessa is NOT from Canada, **from Brazil speaks excellent English**. And said that she was tired of the FBI continuously investigating her because of all of these scammers using her pictures.

Annie calls me once in a while as I look at the call back number, and it is her. As soon as I pick up the telephone, she hangs up. Thomas is not sure what that is all about, and he will not talk to her again, and the emails have abruptly stopped. Although Thomas thanks Annie for getting him started journaling and contacting publishers and began writing books. Annie did note extensively long emails two Thomas that Thomas has quite an education to pass on two others scammed romantically and fraudulently by these ladies.

Thomas doing research, found out that in Canada, romantic scammers get six years in prison and possibly up to 12 years in prison. For instance, in the United States is like a slap on the hand the maximum they can get is two years and possibly a fine. Not Canada.

So, Thomas is excited about putting Annie away with her gigolo, the fiancé to Ginette. Ginette and Thomas are working together to put Annie and her gigolo Mark behind bars: this should not continue, and it will not stop.

So you men out there, be careful: you can fall in love very quickly with a picture and even get telephone calls from these ladies, and they will be so convincing that you are just the man for them. Fortunately for Thomas, it did not cost a lot of money. Thomas only sent computers and iPhones that Annie had sent to Thomas's house. God only knows, receiving and purchasing these computers and iPhones, and Thomas could mail them to New York as Annie would even send Thomas the shipping label. Simply amazing.

Thomas has found a brand-new love, and Ginette loves Thomas. And as this series moves forward, there will be more twists and turns than a pet gofer burrowing throughout his whole and hang on see if you can see which way these critters are going. It is fascinating. And love is unbelievable. The love that Thomas has for God surpasses the imagination or comprehension.

Thomas looks at these souls as lost as he understood that Annie was lying quite a while ago and tried to shine the light so this one lost sheep could find her way. Although greed is a very cunning powerful baffling way, Satan, I'm afraid, has got her soul for eternity going to hell.

That's unfortunate. Sometimes Thomas wonders and just curious why certain people do not have a conscience to decipher the difference between right and wrong and take advantage of others. That's when Thomas finds himself praying I'm praying hard to God, and that's when the miracles happen, such as his new beautiful lady Ginette.

Although hang on for the ride. Smile.

Thomas reaches out to the pornography industry. I am mainly trying to get married men sitting at home, sending these ladies money, thinking that they will get married one day and live happily ever after. Thomas is thinking, give me a break, please. Not one place in the Bible does God say to pray for Satan or forgive him. Thomas is tired of being a doormat.

Thomas has three questions he always asked ladies online, how much money do you have? How old are you? Ladies still lie about that. And how much you weigh? Smile, and ladies indeed lie about that one. Using makes the conversations brief, although impressive.

Thomas does have a great sense of humor and loves to laugh: it keeps him young. Thomas has no regrets or resentments. That is a moment of happiness he will never get back. Insist on enjoying life, Thomas refuses to have one negative moment. And does not take himself too seriously. Stay in the moment: the last minute is gone, the next minute is not here yet, right at this very moment, everything is okay. Okay? It takes practice, although it can be accomplished through the grace of God.

Thomas loves Ginette so much, and she is planning a trip to Arizona state very soon: they are talking about it and even talking about living together. However, Thomas and Ginette are focused on putting Annie and her gigolo away in the Canadian prison, not to do their escapades with others. And destroy other marriages and relationships through romantic fraudulent evil love.

CHAPTER 1

God, Are You Kidding?

Living alone, Thomas finds enjoyment in communicating online in a chat room: if you're not going to provide money for these moral ladies of stature, conversations are brief. Thomas has found over time, and the bottom line is they always want money. You cannot buy love. You cannot control passion, and you cannot own enjoyment, and the very best things in life are free.

Thomas placed his profile on a free Christian website: what Thomas enjoyed about that website is that you could take tests to increase knowledge and wisdom with the Bible. He always knows to accept that Thomas devotes his life to God and service, thinking his soul mate would be in heaven waiting.

One day Thomas minds his own business, taking a test on this website, and this beautiful lady taps Thomas on the shoulder, and as he turned around, she has sent Thomas a full page of communication, not asking for one penny. And Thomas knew instantly after four years of communicating he was in total amazement.

The first thing Thomas said, "God, are you kidding me?" It was like Abraham, 98 years old, in the Bible, getting Sarah pregnant with his wife at the age of 89 years past. And they named their son "Isaac," which means laughter in Hebrew.

Everyone longs to give themselves completely to someone, have a deep soul relationship with another, and be loved thoroughly and exclusively.

Hang on for the unbelievable twist and turns: Thomas lives by Faith and the word of God. (BIBLE - Basic Instructions Before Leaving Earth.) And Thomas will take care of Ginette with respect, compassion, love, understanding, and the Holy Spirit, through Jesus Christ, our Lord.

You will not believe what God has in store for Thomas and Ginette. God condones this union without reservation. A love through prayer, Faith, rigorous indignation, honesty, and trust. You cannot own passion: you cannot control desire: you cannot buy love to obtain that elusive love. Finding yourself letting go, and if it were meant to be, it would come back. A passion is never forgotten, in heaven above where eternally, it is reunited only for those who love.

1 Corinthians 13: 4-8. *Love is patient and kind: love does not envy or boast: it is not arrogant or rude. It does not insist on its way: it is not irritable or resentful: it does not rejoice at wrongdoing but rejoices with the truth. Love bears all things, believes all things, hopes all things, endures all things. Love* never ends. As for prophecies, they will pass away: as for tongues, they will cease: it will move out as for knowledge.

Ginette's friends and acquaintances, along with Thomas's family and friends, have doubts about recognizing Thomas and Ginette's, devoted endless love for one another: Satan will attack this love with a vengeance, if God goes before you, who can be against you?

Joshua 1: 5 – *there shall not any man be able to stand before thee all the days of thy life: as I was with Moses, so I will be with thee: I will not fail thee, nor forsake thee.* Matthew 4: 1 – then was Jesus led up of the spirit into the wilderness to be tempted of the devil. Matthew 4: 7 – *Jesus said unto him, it is written again, thou shall not tempt the Lord thy God.* Matthew 4: 10 – *then saith Jesus unto him, Get thee hence, Satan: for it is written, Thou shalt worship the Lord thy God, and him only shalt thou serve.*

God gave the angels charge over us. Psalms 91: 11 – *for he shall give his angels charge over thee, to keep thee in all thy ways.* Take notice in this verse, "Angels," plural not singular. Meaning every soul has two angels.

But God to the Christian says, "No, not until you're satisfied and fulfilled and content with living, loved by Me alone and giving yourself totally and unreservedly to Me. To have an intensely personal and unique relationship with Me alone.

"I love you, My child, and until you discover that only in Me is your satisfaction to be found, you will not be capable of the perfect human relationship that I have planned for you. You will never unite with another until your combined with Me -- exclusive of anyone or anything else, exclusive of any other desires or belongings.

"I want you to stop planning, stop wishing, and allow Me to bring it to you. You keep watching Me, expecting the most significant things. Keep learning and listening to the things I tell you. You must wait.

"Don't be anxious, and don't worry. Don't look around at the things you think you want. Just keep looking off and away up to Me, or you'll miss what I have to show you.

"And then, when you're ready, I'll surprise you with love far more beautiful than any you would ever dream. You see until you prepared, and until the one I have for you is ready. I am working this minute to have both of you developed at the same time. And until you are both satisfied exclusively with Me and the life I've made for you, you won't be able to experience the love that exemplifies your relationship with Me, and this is perfect love.

"And dear one, I want you to have this most wonderful love. I want you to see in the flesh a picture of your relationship with Me and to enjoy materially and concretely the everlasting union of beauty and perfection and love that I offer you with Myself. Know I love you. I am God Almighty, belief, and be satisfied."

Almost one year of communicating intimately on the computer and increased their communication to the telephone. Her name is Ginette, and she lives in Canada and very intuitive and intelligent.

Any time you can speak two languages fluently, you are one of the sharpest tools in the tool shed, if not the most acute. Ginette knew what she wanted when she made contact, and they communicated.

Keep in mind Thomas has not been with the lady in years. And Thomas informed Ginette that he would inevitably hurt her feelings consciously or unconsciously because he is a man. And that's what men do best is hurt ladies' feelings without knowing.

And Thomas also stated that he is not a millionaire right from the beginning, and if you asked Thomas for any financial support, that would terminate the very brief friendship.

She has respected that request honorably because of her Christian background in being saved through the blood of Jesus Christ, the Lord, and Savior. Ginette has manners, class, morals, a Christian lady with respect: talking to anyone online nowadays makes it hard to find a Christian lady or a Christian man.

Ginette knows the Bible well and talks about God continuously and Jesus Christ, our Lord. Her mother, Diane, also recognizes the Bible very well. Ladies are far more intelligent than men: their intuition, feelings, and emotions make them above and beyond a man's infinite thoughts of being brain-dead. Smile

Let's portray a scenario: if you tell a man that so-and-so died, the man says, "geez, that's too bad." And that's the end of that, and you might as well go down to the river and talk to a rock. Smile, Not a woman, when one of the lady's friends informs her that one of her friends passed on, they cry about it, talk about it, get the support group together, and mourn the occasion. Thank God for ladies, very complicated creation and should be appreciated.

True to Thomas's thoughts, not talking to a lady on Thomas and Ginette's communication level have been communicating. Thomas has hurt her feelings more often than he would care to remember. And that makes him sad: this beautiful lady understands and will not let Thomas go. And for that, he has commended her for being the gracious lady that she is: for that simple misunderstood reason.

Thomas would not be the man he is today without Ginette: she has changed Thomas's life in ways that he could not have ever thought of, and Ginette has brought more miracles into their lives as far as compatibility goes. And they will be listed as we get further into this manuscript.

Nothing happens perchance, and Ginette's mother, Diane, Ginette, and Thomas, were praying for the same thing. Thomas prays to God that Ginette and her mother will continue to hold Thomas's expectations to an introductory level. Smile, God willing, Thomas is exceptionally excited about this relationship, or should he say marriage?

CHAPTER 2

Thomas

Thomas, born in Arizona, lived the life of extremes. Thomas is the eldest, and at present, Thomas and his two brothers and two sisters. Growing up hard, we had to work for everything to keep food on the table. Being the eldest, Thomas feels incredibly blessed, raised in a loving family, only through God's Grace and the family's Faith.

Thomas, his brothers, and sisters will join the family later, not just yet.

Thomas's memoirs prove God's mercy, miracles in the time of hell. Thomas finds himself dancing with the devil, doing a little soft shoe, tripping to the light fantastic, and doing the Boogaloo, then bidding the devil farewell. Thomas has a lot of work to do for God: he is still behind the eight ball. Thomas was relieved of the mental obsession and the physical compulsion of drugs and alcohol through a miraculous prayer.

Thomas admits to destroying relationships through drugs and alcohol abuse. He now has six years clean and sober and still witnesses miracles and experiences them from a loving God.

He owned and operated his businesses, attended college. Thomas enjoying life, refuses to have one negative moment of worry or stress because he will never get back a moment of happiness. Living alone, ironic, drinking and drugging his way through life and relationships, and at present living, single. Not that the opportunity has not arisen or became available.

When he buys a pair of shoes, Thomas's belief does not try them on: first, he buys them, takes them home, and has the unshakable faith that they will fit. In other words, fornication or adultery is not right in the eyes of God. We only come: this way once: this time, Thomas intends on doing it the Christian way. God's gift to us his life: what we do with this life is our gift to God.

A stern believer in Christianity, God, Jesus Christ, our Lord and Savior, the Holy Spirit, Angels, Saints, Bible, and experiencing miracles of biblical proportion.

Thomas has never known love, it has just been a feeling or an emotion, and there's more to love than just that. It is caring for another to give yourself to that other person through God's Grace,

Prayer, Bible, Jesus Christ, Holy Spirit, Sharing, Caring, Loving, kindness, compassion, intimacy, sensual, and sexual love.

That only God could offer through the Holy Spirit, eternally. Thomas has learned that there is love, far more significant and much more in-depth than any human couple or couples could have ever imagined or experienced, the love of God.

And to experience the growth of love that stretches from sky to sky, and all the oceans cannot hold the depths of love. This love has no beginning or no end: This love comes from another dimension revealed from the Holy Spirit through Thomas and Ginette's writings and communication together. And reading slowly and patiently, understand a love never experienced that comes directly from God our holy father, Jesus Christ our Lord, and the Holy Spirit.

This is a miraculous love that every man woman to come to realize there's a gift for them far beyond their comprehension or imagination. Thomas and Ginette have learned how to tap into this love, only through the Grace of God.

It's a new and exciting feeling, caring and loving for another, and it just keeps getting better: it keeps growing abundantly with every new day. More shall be revealed through this powerful and exciting new love.

It is saving the best for last, meeting Ginette online at a Christian dating site. It is like an elusive dream that you thought could never come true, only to find out that it is real and can be obtainable with a boundless love that will never stop growing. Thomas will love that woman and take care of her, as he has never loved before.

Thomas dreams about this love from time to time at night, and it's a feeling Thomas has never experienced. So hang on for love you will want to have and never let go, is meant to inspire couples: this love is for real. And it is available to everyone, all you have to do is ask with Faith, and you shall receive. Through God's timing, not ours, he is patiently waiting a lifetime, beyond Thomas's comprehension or imagination. Thinking Thomas's soul mate was in heaven was the greatest injustice Thomas has committed to his mind until Thomas started praying. John 14: 27. -*"I am leaving you with a gift- peace of mind and heart. And the peace I give as a gift the world cannot provide. So don't be troubled or afraid."*

CHAPTER 3

Ginette

Ginette born in Canada: her father was from the island of Malta off the southern tip of Italy. Ginette's dad passed on when she 14 years young, and she grew without a father in her life. With no brothers and sisters. As a result, Ginette was an orphan from that age on, and her mother is a widow.

Her mother, Diane, is a very gracious, God-fearing, beautiful lady, with wisdom and knowledge, such as her daughter. Ginette and her mother, Diane, speak fluent French, and only Ginette speaks English very well. Ginette is a very hard-working lady and, at one point in time, modeled for Tiffany. Ginette now lives in Canada.

Ginette works in an exquisite restaurant. Ginette works very long hours, from 8 a.m. until 8 p.m., waitressing tables six days a week. A lovely, beautiful, God-fearing lady with wisdom and kindness attends the Baptist Church and proclaims Christianity.

Ginette conveyed that her first boyfriend in high school beat her quite often: Ginette is not seeking another abusive relationship. She was saved through Jesus Christ, our Lord, and holds a strong moral belief in Christianity. Ginette's mother Diane and Ginette plan a trip to Malta and then on to Paris, France. Ginette's mother speaks little English and will feel comfortable in France. Ginette's family consists of her mother and herself, and they have adopted Thomas into their small nucleus of a family.

Ginette in an automobile accident when she was learning how to drive and crashed her Father's care: as a result of her knees on occasion, the pain is so severe she has to go into a hospital to receive extreme pain medication to relieve the pain.

Ginette has not been in a relationship for three years and pursues a Christian man on dating sites to no avail. Ginette is aware of her girlfriends her age, the broken relationships that they get into with men. Ginette's intuition, knowledge, and wisdom seek to find a gentleman who will treat her with respect, love, and kindness. Ginette, never married or has any children, can settle down and become a homemaker and take care of the family.

Ginette, her mother, and Thomas have been praying, and prayer is powerful medicine: Jesus left us with three gifts. 1, to cast out evil spirits, 2, the laying on of hands to heal, 3, the Holy Spirit that moves throughout the earth, answering prayers, and between us, helping one another with lovingkindness.

Out of 7.7 billion people on this planet, God has Blessed Ginette and Thomas, answering their prayers along with Ginette's mother. Psalm 91:11. *For he shall give his angels charge over thee, to keep thee in all thy ways.* Thomas feels he has been assigned a guardian angel through the miraculous communion with Ginette.

The best way to determine what God wants for you in your relationship and life is to seek Him. Pray to God for wisdom concerning your marriage. The only way to learn if you're making the right choice is by aligning yourself with the one who created you. Only then can you understand what God wants for you. No one else can tell you what is best for you than God through the power of the Holy Spirit.

Love knows no age, while people who date others much younger or older than them owe no one an explanation.

"Then he (Boaz) said, 'May you be blessed of the LORD, my daughter. You have shown your last kindness to be better than the first by not going after young men, whether poor or rich" (Ruth 3:10).

In searching the Bible for documented marriages, we don't find any that can sway us in an accurate direction or give us an idea of what God may be leading us to. The only warning regarding marriage age is to avoid marrying someone young for lustful purposes and avoid marrying someone older for money.

CHAPTER 4

Romance

Thomas finds himself attracted to Ginette with a romantic pull is so powerful and strong, knowing this came with the love of God, through his holy grace. Thomas is madly in love with Ginette. Thomas loves Ginette so much that it makes Thomas's heart hurt with such a magnetic passion.

Suppose you are a man and indeed a God-fearing man and yourself in the presence of a God-fearing lady. These spiritual gifts within you will be as rubies to her and treat her with kindness. Nurture her, do not defile her, communicate, love, respect her, and walk-in her shoes. Feel her feelings, have symphony for her compassion, given her freedom, and protect her make her feel secure. She'll make you worth living the life God has chosen for the two of you. Hold her high publicly, tell her how proud and you love her unconditionally. Anything less, her intuition and God's Holy Spirit, will make you humble to your knees, begging.

Her heart is broken when the next of kin or friend dies. But she finds the strength to get on with life. She knows that a kiss and a hug can heal a broken heart.

There is only one thing wrong with her: she forgets what she is worth.

Ginette's sweetness is unsurpassable by candies, and flowers cannot compete with her fragrant scent, a beautiful lady created by God. Ginette is a tasty little morsel, a gorgeous crêpe Suzette, a passionate flaming soufflé, baked Alaska, a luscious, sumptuous, custard pudding with French vanilla whipping cream, pumpkin pie with French vanilla banana split ice cream, cherries Jubilee, while slowly pouring chocolate and raspberry syrup, and a delicious, delightful flavor. Exquisitely sumptuously luscious and pleasing to the palate.

That Thomas patiently will take his time to savor this sweet flavor from the North Country. Ginette and Thomas give praise to the Lord, the MasterChef God Almighty. Thank you for being real, honest, and trustworthy: Thomas loves Ginette beyond words. Every day Thomas finds himself drawn one step deeper in love.

Thomas will never grow weary of being with Ginette. My sweet, precious heavenly Guardian

Angel, I will always love you. You took my breath away the first time I looked into your heart and realized that you are one beautiful lady sent from above, as one unique spirit. There's nothing single about being together with you. With you, tomorrow is inevitably precious.

When we are together tenderly kissing, I love you dearly, creating lasting and unforgettable memories. Together we have a unique love. Much more, Thomas desires to partake with Ginette, today and forever. I will cherish you forever.

Before Thomas met Ginette, my precious Guardian Angel treasure from the North country, Thomas's life was miserable. Now Thomas has the God-given opportunity to make up for those lost years by spending and to cherish every moment with Ginette. I love you so much.

There's no law, time, reason, or idea holding back Thomas's secure love for Ginette. Thomas does not have any restrictions. I love you so much, only through God's holy miraculous precious Grace, more than Ginette could ever imagine.

Ginette means everything to Thomas. Thomas finds that letting Ginette do precisely what she wants to do when she wants to do it, and who she cares to show loving kindness.

Just a side note for you gentlemen: "(Arguing with your wife is like trying to blow out a light bulb. If she wants you to change the diapers, do it, John Wayne. If she wants you to wash the dishes, do it, Willie Nelson. If she wants you to vacuum and clean the house, do it, Brad Pitt. If she wants you to go to the opera, do it, Arnold Schwarzenegger.)"

Proceeding forward with love for Ginette, Thomas has found happiness, joy, peace, and contentment.

Some say love hurts, but with Ginette, Thomas will be glad to take any risk to be with Ginette. Thomas cherishes the thought of spending the rest of his life with Ginette as his soulmate.

Thomas cannot even envision or imagine what his life would be like without Ginette. I love you, dearly, through amazing Grace with God's love that has no beginning with no end. Together we have learned to tap into this amazing agape love.

With Ginette, Thomas feels integrity, honesty, and trust, Glorious and excellent. Ginette and Thomas are indeed meant to be before their eyes even sparkled into each other's souls. Beyond words, Thomas fell in love with Ginette, before Thomas was blessed, finally granted the opportunity through the Grace of God, to supernaturally come together with Ginette. I will love you, my precious Angel, softly, tenderly, and gently with care and sensual compassion.

Ginette's prophecy: God's amazing Grace: before Thomas and Ginette were born, God created this miraculous union. Thomas will always love Ginette and care for their love. Thomas will cherish Ginette forever. Only with Thomas will Ginette feel safe.

There's nothing impossible about Thomas's goals and aspirations. Thomas will love Ginette, tenderly, with sensual compassion, that neither Thomas nor Ginette has ever known.

Our love's spiritual electricity, Ginette with Thomas, devoting their life to God in-service, will experience an overabundance of blessings. They have already discovered the pot of gold at the end of the rainbow.

As long as they live by the word of God and pray together, no harsh word between the two of them. As stated in the Lord's prayer, "on earth as it is in heaven." For the miraculous union that God has brought them together. Ginette and Thomas's prayer: is that through their writings, they can reach out and get thousands of souls into the light of heaven's gate.

From every human being, there rises a light that reaches straight to heaven, and when Thomas and Ginette's souls are destined to find each other together, their streams of light flowed together, and a single brighter light goes forth from them. United being you were born together, and together you shall be forever said the Lord.

Have powerful dreams and goals—for yourself, each other, and the marriage. You need ideas to keep you genuinely alive and vital. They help you create passion: for life and each other.

Every day, find a way to show appreciation to people you love and people who give you service. It also includes clerks, salespeople, wait staff, people who hold doors open, people who let you in traffic, etc. "Thank you" is the universal currency that pays BIG dividends.

Say, "I Love You" to each other at least once a day! This is another way to say, "Thank you." Use both phrases. They multiply each other by at least ten! Do little things for each other, and you increase the effect by one hundred! Never go to bed angry with each other because talking it out will save you time, energy, and mistakes the next day.

The number one key to a successful marriage or relationship is the Bible. Continuously forgive each other. Problems of a marriage or relationship, lack communication, arguing over money, being unfaithful and untrustworthy.

Matthew 6: 12. – *And forgive us our debts, as we forgive our debtors. 14. For if you forgive men their trespasses, your heavenly Father will also forgive you.* [15]. *But if you forgive not men their trespasses, neither will your Father forgive your trespasses.*

Thomas and Ginette pray from their hearts, with love, that forgiveness and asking for God's will. I am the light says the Lord, he who follows Me will never be in darkness: Thomas and Ginette love, Jesus Christ! This is their prayer for you today. 1 John 4 16 – 21 –*And we have known and believed the love that God has for us. God is love: he that dwells in love dwells in God and God in him. Here is our love made perfect, that we may have boldness in the day of judgment: because as He is, so are we in this world. We love Him because he first loved us. If a man says, I love God, and hates his brother: he is a liar: for he loves not his brother who he has seen, how can he love God who he has not seen? And this commandment has we from Him that he who loves God loves his brother also.*

Souls who never thought that God could or would work in our lives, those who pray together, stay together. Thomas and Ginette are Christians and only through God's amazing miraculous Grace and praise the Lord Jesus Christ.

Perfection is a set-up for disappointment. This is not the Garden of Eden, and everything happens for a reason: giving and receiving is a two-way street. Why so-called bad situations happen to good people is because God loves us that much. When a harmful problem occurs in your life, and life shows up, there will be more useful coming from that than terrible. God's way of showing us his love, God's will not ours, be done. Revelation 3: 19 – *As many as I love, I rebuke and chastise, be zealous therefore and repent.*

Please learn to handle constructive criticism and accept your age of accountability. Blasphemy of the Holy Spirit, through spiritual discernment, letting others know with courage, what they are doing, or saying, is not right in the eyes of God. For instance, if someone damns God in front of you, please inform them that they are breaking the third commandment. "Thou shalt not use the Lord's name in vain."

If there are couples you know living together in fornication without being married, it would be a graceful way to let them know: that the lady would feel more secure in the relationship if she were married. God's children will be judged on what they think, what they say, what they do, and what they fail to do.

1 Corinthians 7: 2. –*Nevertheless, to avoid fornication, let every man have his wife, and let every woman have her husband.*

1 Corinthians 6: 18. –*Flee fornication. Every sin that a man doeth is without the body, but he that committeth fornication sinneth against his own body.*

Everybody else is doing it, and money can buy your amusement, but not happiness: money can buy the best doctors. Still, only God can heal you, money can buy you the best food, but only God can give you the appetite to enjoy it, money can buy you a house, but not a home.

Happiness is sitting on your back porch, watching your children and grandchildren screaming all around you. There are two types of people in this world, those who bow down to everything in it as their God or those who bow down to Jesus Christ to get to God.

No one comes to the Father, but by me, says Jesus Christ, our Lord, and Savior. John 8: 19. *Then said they unto him, Where is thy Father? Jesus answered, Ye, neither know me nor my Father: if ye had known me, ye should have known my Father also.*

To test the spirit of the truth: The unbelievers of the truth do not want examination. If you criticize the unbelievers of validity, you expose their error if you pursue to contend for the truth. They will turn it around and condemn you as a sinner.

If this is the real work of the Holy Spirit, they would be inviting all the scrutiny they could get if they were honest and trustworthy? They would want the authentication if they were correct?

They are deceitful and fraudulent in the Errors of their ways. You are the one standing in their way of the truth, in the Bible, and the teachings of Jesus. For them to succeed, they have to turn inequity into a transgression against Christ. Sound doctrine proves that they do not survive.

Proverbs 6:16-19, *"There are six things the LORD hates, seven that are detestable to him. Haughty eyes, a lying tongue, hands that shed innocent blood, a heart that devises wicked schemes, feet that are quick to rush into evil, a false witness who pours out lies, and a man who stirs up dissension among brothers."*

If you are a lady and invited out on a dinner date with your new gentleman/boyfriend? This man is trying to impress this lovely young lady and proceeds to entertain her at an exquisite restaurant. Arriving at this elegant restaurant's front door, they met at the front entrance and were led into the restaurant by the maître d'. Who greets this couple with ethical morality and politeness and seats them at their table. It seems to be heaven on earth when brought there drinks hors d'oeuvres and dinner salad placed in front of them.

This gentleman does not even thank God for this beautiful lady or this bounty: they are about to eat. The first thing this so-called gentleman does is picks up his fork and start eating before the lady.

Whenever you go out to dinner with the man, And he eats: first, this lady may decide to look elsewhere without any ethical manners, kindness, or consideration.

This egotistical man could also be selfish (reflective love of self) 10% of all humans are born with some narcissistic character defect. And their habits have never found a known cure. Very similar to Satan, who thought he was better than God, the reason Michael and his archangels threw Satan out of heaven.

He is putting on a show just for the sole purpose of trying to impress this sweet, beautiful lady, anything that he thinks she wants to hear or do, for the sole purpose of getting his way with her.

"A God thought." Thomas, Watching this television program about two Belgium German shepherds separated while the owners moved across two states. The husband-wife and two children were moving for the reason the husband transferred at his work. The company was paying for the move: although the husband could not be late for work, he had to make the appointment scheduled.

In a station wagon, the wife two children and two German shepherds. About 200 miles into their journey, while at a rest stop, the male German Shepherd wandered down the swiftly moving river trail and did not notice the families' despair and urgency. The family looked desperately but could not find this majestic male best friend. The family looked and called for this male Belgium Shepherd.

They had to leave after an extensive rapid search with others. They were placing notices on bulletin boards and even an ad in a local newspaper. When they arrived at their new home, the male German Shepherd traveled about 200 miles before hooking up with the family. Two days after the family came into their new home, a commotion and barking from the female German Shepherd, as the male German Shepherd, scratched at their home's front door.

To this family, it was that as though one of their children had been lost and miraculously found. There was so much excitement, happiness, and joy within the household.

This male German Shepherd had lost about 10 pounds, and his paws bloodied, and he did not look well, although happy to be in the company of familiar spirits. They put a bowl of water and food out for him, but he would not drink water or eat until the female ate first—characteristic of this male German Shepherd dog.

Ginette commented: Wow, that's an effortless way to tell if a man loves, from the German Shepherd story. You can see even animals, knows the male is supposed to look after his female partner, if men had such characteristic like that dog, then there's no reason why their females wouldn't love them back. I hope you're like that German Shepherd! My heart tells me you have excellent quality, and you are indeed the man of my dream.

You touch essential points, and I sit here to take my time and reading and taking in so much than you think: you are full of wisdom. And those that read your books would save their lives. You make touching points that would bring a dying person back to life, and I'm so blessed to have such a person in my life. At least

I wouldn't be a reader, but hearing from you directly, as we live together.

Thomas commented:

Peace and Grace of the Lord be with you and your mother through Jesus Christ, our Lord name amen hugs and kisses with love, prayers, kindness, care, consideration, and precious heavenly love.

Ginette has been captivated through God's Grace and both of their unshakable Faith. And agape a love that is as deeper than all the oceans and stretches from sky to sky. This love has no beginning or no end. The perfect love can be accomplished without one harsh word, only through the word of God. Making love and having sex between married couples is God's idea. Read the Song of Solomon, a short book in the Bible.

Song of Solomon 4: 5 – *your two breasts are like two fawns, Twins of a gazelle, that graze among the lilies.* Song of Solomon 4: 11 – *your lips drip nectar, my bride: honey and milk are under your tongue: the fragrance of your garments is like the fragrance of Lebanon.* Song of Solomon 4: 13 – *your shoots are an orchard of pomegranates with all choicest fruits, camphire with spikenard.* Song of Solomon 4: 16 – *she awake, O North-wind, and come O South-wind! Blow upon my garden, let its spices flow. Let my beloved come to his garden and eat its choicest fruits.*

The above exchange was between Solomon and his bride. This is a very erotic moment that some will shy away from due to its sexual and sensual nature. It is romantic poetry, and this is foreplay, and God is encouraging it. Song of Solomon 5:1 – *eat, friends, drink, and be drunk with love.*

The Scripture above can be concluded, and "potentially" says about sex is good. God thought of everything. The Song of Solomon is an erotic book between a husband and his wife. And if you're married, this concise book in the Bible should be read one to another when married. Consensually, in a romantic mood, it can enhance the sensual sexual atmosphere. Thus, if done in any fashion outside of marriage or without mutual consent, it is a sin. And an abomination against God, and not one omen shall go unpaid owed to God, and every soul will be held accountable. What God intended for our pleasure, we must not abuse. For one day, Thomas and Ginette will have children together, God willing.

CHAPTER 5

Coincidence? Or God's Loving Grace?

Ginette's birthday is the same day and month as Thomas's Father's. Thomas's dad's first name and Ginette's dad's first name are the same. Spelled differently but pronounced the same.

Thomas and Ginette are both first fruits (firstborn) devoting their lives sacrificially to God and helping others. They keep God first, say their prayers together, devoting their lives to God in- service helping others.

Ginette and Thomas's childhood hero is Zorro. Ginette's favorite color is purple, and Thomas's favorite color is blue. They complement one another.

Thomas and Ginette both look-alike, and they both have dimples when they smile, and you can see the joy and happiness of the Holy Spirit and love in their smiles. A day without laughter is a day without sunshine. Thomas and Ginette always have a smile on their face.

Ginette's mother, Diane, and Thomas's mother gave birth to Thomas and Ginette at 20.

Ginette's mother, Diane being a non-Catholic, married a Catholic husband. Thomas's mother, being a non-Catholic, married a Catholic husband. Ginette and Thomas are planning to become married, God willing. Thomas raised a Catholic, and Ginette grew a Baptist. Ginette, a non-Catholic, will be marrying a Catholic man.

Thomas sings karaoke, recorded a song he had written, and sent it to Ginette: Ginette let her mother Diane listen. And according to Diane, Thomas sounds exactly like her favorite singer, "Kenny Rogers."

Ginette, Thomas, and Diane complement one another: Ginette a Baptist, Thomas a Catholic, and Diane a charismatic. Just so happened they were called home at the same time and arrived at heaven's gates, where Saint Peter greeted them. St. Peter said, "your mansions are just not quite ready yet: you will have to wait. So St. Peter called Satan, and ask Satan, could keep them for a couple of days. Satan agreed: after one day, Satan called St. Peter and said, "You have to get them out of there immediately." Ginette the Baptist is saving people, Thomas the Catholic his forgiving people, and Diane the charismatic has raised enough money to put air conditioning down here.

Only through God's Grace can these many similarities come together between Ginette and Thomas. Thomas and Ginette devote their lives to God in-service, along with Ginette's mother, Diane. The key to accepting a successful marriage continuously forgive each other, communicate with one another consistently with love. Thomas and Ginette store their riches in heaven, not of this earth. God only mentions this once in the Bible. John chapter 15: 13 – *there is no greater love than this, that one should lay down their life for their friend or neighbor.* This is the unconditional love that one would give their life for their friend.

Thomas should get called home before Ginette, and Thomas has made Ginette promise that she will remarry another Christian. Thomas and Ginette have both agreed, according to the Bible.

1 Corinthians: 7: 39 – *the wife is bound by the law as long as her husband lives, but if her husband is dead, she is at liberty to be married to whom she will, only in the Lord.*

Through God's Holy Grace and Jesus Christ, our Lord's name through the Holy Spirit, God answered Thomas's prayer along with Ginette's mother Diane, and Ginette.

Ginette has turned Thomas around in his battle with pornography online. And for a man without a lady, this is extremely addictive and evil. And in the eyes of God is an abomination pertaining directly to fornication and adultery.

If Ginette came into Thomases life for no other reason than to save his soul, the union well worth it to God.

A single man living alone would inherently and absorb this character defect into his DNA spiritually. Does Thomas feel other men can relate to the devil's pull spiritually on the soul from watching pornography?

It may not seem like an addiction or anything to be concerned about. I beg the difference, and it is an addiction being very cunning powerful, and baffling. And it may seem very easy to break if you are married to your wife, not knowing.

Just because you men are married and watching pornography. Even though men feel that there is nothing wrong with the appearance of other ladies. Wrong, wrong, wrong, the seventh commandment. "Thou shalt not commit adultery." Impaired thinking, Satan can justify the means to where you think it is perfectly okay. And all of a sudden you are in hell for eternity.

Just because you're married does not mean you can watch pornography. And get aroused, and then have sex with your wife. Thinking you entirely satisfy her. And relating it to improving your marriage. Wrong, wrong wrong.

It's an abomination against God and will NOT get your soul to heaven.

And it will lead you eventually astray. Keep in mind that mass murderers started out watching pornography. Ted Bundy, Jeffrey Dahmer. Just a couple off the top of my head. Jim Jones, the Jamestown massacre in Africa.

A very evil lousy addiction, and Thomas finds it repulsive to even think of pornography anymore. Or even think of another lady, in his thinking or his mind.

Matthew 5: 28 – *But I say unto you. That whosoever looks on a woman to lust after committing adultery with her, already in his heart.* 1 John 2: 16 – *For all that is in the world, the lust of the flesh and the desire of the eyes, and the pride of life, is not of the Father, but is of the world.*

Through meeting Ginette online, Thomas is also in the process of fixing up a house and trying to make it a very comfortable home for Ginette and her mother. Very majestic settings amongst "God's country."

Thomas continuously reads the Bible, and that is an addiction that Thomas finds himself studying the Bible 8, possibly 10 hours a day. And more shall be revealed.

Romans 14: 10 – 13. *Why do you pass judgment on your brother? Or you, why do you despise your brother? For we will all stand before the judgment seat of God: for it is written, "As I live, says the Lord, every knee shall bow to me, and every tongue shall confess to God."* So then each of us will give an account of himself to God. Therefore let us not pass judgment on one another any longer, but rather decide never to put a stumbling block or hindrance in the way of a brother. Not one omen owed to God shall go unpaid. Luke 6: 37. *"Judge not, and you will not be judged: condemn not, and you will not be doomed: forgive, and you will be forgiven:*

A passion is never forgotten in heaven above, where eternally, it is reunited, only for the ones who love." 1 Peter 3: 7. *Likewise, ye wives, be in subjection to your husbands: if any open a not the word, they also may without the word be won by the wives' conversation.*

Respect and obey your husbands in the same way. Then the husbands, who do not follow the word of God, will want to know God. They will want to know God because their wives live useful lives, even though they say nothing about God. They will see that you live holy lives and respect your husbands.

Ginette and her mother, Diane, traveling abroad: this does not disrupt Thomas and Ginette's communication daily and enhance their love for one another together.

When one of them is not feeling well, it seems to be the other one is not either. They are most certainly equally yoked spiritually.

One could not put this many coincidences together, only through their Faith, prayers, and love for God. And the supernatural Grace of God, answering prayers before they were born.

Ginette, Diane, and Thomas keep God first, say their prayers, devoting their lives to God in-service helping others, proceed forward on that narrow path to heaven. Piece and Grace of the Lord be with you, your family, and friends through Jesus Christ, our Lord's name amen.

When your day is long and the night is yours alone. When you're sure you've had enough of this life, well hang on, don't let yourself go, because everybody cries and everybody hurts sometimes. Sometimes everything is wrong, everybody hurts, so take comfort in your friends, everybody cries sometimes, and everybody sometimes hurts, so hold on, you're not alone.

An Eternal Gift Through God's Grace, Inspired to store my riches in heaven having nothing of worldly gratification.

And I thank God from heaven above for the Souls I genuinely love. We will possibly come together again one day, although not yet.

II Corinthians 5: 8: *"To be absent from the flesh, is to be present with the Lord."*

John 14:27, *"I am leaving you with a gift-peace of mind and heart. And the peace I give is a gift the world cannot provide. So don't be troubled or afraid."*

The untold story of Amazing Grace.

This song, "Amazing Grace," performed by a stunning tenor voice of an African-American Singer on stage, made this statement in a New York City concert auditorium.

He never said who the slave trader was—a slave trader in writing the most celebrated gospel hymn in Christianity's history. "Amazing grace, how sweet the sound." written by one of the most sinful men who ever lived," certainly John Newton was."

A slave trader, while bringing slaves from Africa to America, would hear the suffering souls that were in the bowels of the ship. When they would get together, and they would sing, he said, "it was a mournful tune of suffering because they were leaving their homes, and going to a life of uncertainty. And many of them experiencing cruelty beyond description, but the melody burned into John Newton's mind.

When John Newton got saved, "he said I was a great sinner, but I met a great Savior, how sweet the sound That saved a wretch like me, I once was lost, but now I am found, was blind but now I see.

And God forgave me of all of my sins. John Newton put his pen to parchment, and the tune was the tune that he had heard coming from the mouths of those suffering. Amazing Grace, how sweet the sound.

And then he made a statement, Thomas had never heard before, and when you have been around as long as Thomas has, and you hear something you've never heard before.

It would help if you listened to this because you can play every note on the amazing Grace piano, "only on the black keys."

The song Amazing Grace is sacred, and it was born out of suffering that a generation, after generation, after age. That the Grace of God has no limit, there is no limit to the Grace of God. Just a sidebar to you millennials trying to invent a new melody to go with those words, back off and forget it, and leave the song along.

CHAPTER 6

Widow and Orphan: Is God, In Holy Habitation.

Ginette's Father called home when Ginette was 14 years young, which made Ginette fatherless or an orphan and made her mother a widow. They are leaving themselves vulnerable to predators and not trusting men because they are continuously being taken advantage of by these ungodly predators.

Exodus 22: 22 – *you shall not afflict any widow or illegitimate child. Zachariah 7: 10 – and oppress not the widow, nor the fatherless, the stranger, nor the poor: and that none of you imagine evil against his brother in your heart.*

James 1: 27 – *peer religion and undefiled before God and the Father is this. To visit the fatherless and widows in their affliction and to keep himself unspotted from the world. Matthew 23: 14 – woe unto you, scribes and Pharisees, hypocrites! For you, devour widow's houses, and for a pretense make more extended prayer: therefore, you shall receive the greater damnation.*

Isaiah 10: 2 –. *To turn aside the needy from judgment, and to take away the right from the poor of my people, that widows may be there pray, and that they may rob the fatherless! Jeremiah 49: 11 – leave the orphan children, I will preserve them alive, and let the widows trust in me, says the Lord. Psalms 68: 5 – a father of the fatherless and the widows' judge is God in his holy habitation.*

There is no higher honor in the Bible, for the care of widows and orphans, with reverence from God and his amazing Grace. Neither Ginette nor her mother, Diane, has ever had a man in their life, that has not tried to take advantage of them. Thomas looks forward to providing and protecting, with love.

For a reason, this is God's will and the answer to Thomas, Ginette, and her mother Diane's prayers. If for the only reason, Thomas and Ginette come together to become just friends when they first meet. And not for marriage or children. In the theater of their minds, through being apart, communicating continuously.

Ruth: 1 – 16 – *And Ruth said, intreat me not to leave thee, or to return from following after thee: for whither thou goest, I will go: and where thou lodgest, I will lodge: thy people shall be my people, and thy God my God:* *[17] Where thou diest, will I die, and there will I be buried: the Lord do so to me, and more also if aught but death part thee and me.*

A Similar relationship between Ginette and her mother, Diane. Ginette, an orphan, and Diane, a widow, a mother-daughter relationship with a bond never broken.

It makes Thomas as generous as Boaz, and Thomas will ask Ginette's mother, Diane, for Ginette's hand in marriage. When and only if, God willing, the time is appropriate.

Thomas's mother called home, and one thing Thomas misses is not being able to show his mother the love he wished he would have. Thomas loved his mother, although until your mother is called home, you will never know the feeling of not being able to do more.

Thomas has this opportunity to show reverence, kindness, consideration with love to Ginette's mother, Diane, for she is a widow. And this would give Thomas a chance to make amends to his mother, with love and the Grace of God. Through Jesus Christ our Lord, and the Holy Spirit that moves throughout the earth, Thomas's Faith answers prayer.

For we all stand in final, eternal judgment, of what we think, of what we say, what we do, and what we failed to do. And failing to do more: is one defective human characteristic we all have in common—God's gift to us his life. What we do with this life is our gift to God. If you care to make, God laugh, plan your life!

Romans 3: 23 – *For all have sinned, and come short of the glory of God.* 1 Corinthians 7: 29 – *But this I say, brethren, that the time is temporary: it remaineth, that both they that have wives be as though they had none.*

CHAPTER 7

Convincing Proof That God Exists

History "His Story"

Proof of God: If the earth were significantly closer or farther away from the sun, it would not be capable of supporting much of the life it currently does. If the atmosphere elements were even a few percentage points different, nearly every living thing on earth would die. The odds of a single protein molecule forming by chance is one in 10 to the 243rd. (that is a one followed by 243 zeros). A single cell is comprised of millions of protein molecules.

The earth is orbiting the sun departs from a straight line by only one-ninth of an inch every 18 miles – a very straight line in human terms. If the orbit changed by 1/10 of an inch every 18 miles, it would be vastly more extensive, and we would all freeze to death. If a change by 1/8 of an inch, we would be incinerated. The sun is burning at approximately 20,000,000°C at its interior. If the earth were moved 10% further away, we would soon freeze to death.

If it were moved 10% closer, we would be reduced to ashes. Are we to believe that such precision ("just happened"? Think about it: the sun is poised and 93 million miles from earth, which happens to be just right. Did this happen perchance or by design? It's no small wonder that the psalmist alludes to God as a grand designer: *"The heavens declare the glory of God: the skies proclaim the work of his hands. (The sun) rises at one end of the heavens and makes its circuit to the other".* (Psalm 91:1, 6).

Albert Einstein, acknowledged, that there's a master designer of the universe (God). He stated, "I just cannot figure out how he did it." Right then, Albert Einstein humbled himself, realizing that there is something far more significant, far beyond his comprehension. That has an attachment to us eternally, through Faith, known as our soul. We either walk by Faith, or we walk by sight? Fear knocked, Faith answered, no one was there.

His church and each one of those prophecies were fulfilled! The Old Testament contains 48 prophecies that pertain to the birth, life, crucifixion, resurrection, the future described by John the

21

Revel-later, the second coming of Jesus Christ our Lord. When applying the laws of probability to calculate the likelihood of several events taking place at or near the same time, our possibilities have multiplied together. For example, if the likelihood of a single event occurred randomly is one chance in five, the probability of a separate event occurring is 10, which yields one in 50.

Because several different prophets who lived in separate communities over 1000 years made predictions of Christ 500 years before his birth, the odds against these prophecies coming true are simply beyond our wildest comprehension. For example, the chances of one man (Jesus) fulfilling just eight of the prophecies attributed to him are one in 10 to the 17th power. (That is a number one with 17 zeros).

Through the church, believers are taught to obey the Lord and testify concerning their faith in Christ as Savior and honor Him by holy living. We believe in the great commission as a primary mission of the church. All believers should witness, by word and Faith, to the truths of God's word. The gospel of the Grace of God is to preach to all the world. (Matthew 29: 19 – 20. Acts 1: 8:. 2 Corinthians 5: 19 – 20).

Every culture throughout history has had some form of law. Everyone has a sense of right and wrong. Murder, lying, stealing, and immorality are almost universally rejected. Where did this sense of right and wrong come from if not from a holy God?

God gave the angels charge over us. Psalms 91: 11 – *for he shall give his angels charge over thee, to keep thee in all thy ways.* Take notice in this verse, "Angels," plural not singular. Meaning every soul has two angels.

In the end, God's existence must be accepted by faith (Hebrews 11: 6). Faith in God is not a blind leap into the dark: it is a safe step into a well-lit room where the vast majority of people are already standing. This results in the standard error of demanding direct, miraculous, personal revelation. This is the "if God when showing me a miracle, I would believe" approach. Or the "if God would write John 3: 16 on the moon" approach. Jesus warned against such unbelief in Matthew 12: 39. *"A wicked and adulterous generation as for a sign!"*

The Bible, with all its fulfilled prophecies, proves the existence of God. Through the law of probability in the mathematical audits of prophecy being fulfilled, we can know assuredly that there was a divine designer and author of the Bible. The same one who brought the Universe into existence. "You may say to yourselves, " How can we know when the Lord has not spoken a message?" If what a prophet proclaims in the name of the Lord does not take place or come true, that is a message the Lord has not spoken. That prophet has spoken presumptuously". (Deuteronomy 18: 21– 22).

You are personally experiencing miracles of the biblical proportion of the mind and witnessing and listening to two testimony of others of miraculous and unexplained holy incidences of God's prices divine Grace. Have you been to war? You do not know whether you will live from one minute to the next, and the most ardent atheist find themselves praying faithfully, saying statements such as. "God, please help to survive one more day."

There are two types of people in this world, those who bow down to everything in it as their God or those who bow down to Jesus Christ to get to God. No one comes to the Father, but by me, says Jesus Christ, our Lord, and Savior. John 8: 19. Then said they unto him, Where is thy Father? Jesus answered, Ye, neither know me nor my Father: if ye had known me, ye should have known my Father also.

Six million sperm cells swim for one egg, and we make it, a generation before generation, chances of winning the lottery 1000 times daily would be the odds of us being here right now. It seems to be a little too much harmony and order throughout the solar system and the unknown Universe even to consider this to have evolved perchance or coincidently.

We live on 13 plates of molten lava, like living on a cracked egg. And the earth that we think is a solid foundation (crust or 13 separate plates floating on molten lava, on average, the earth's crust is 40 miles thick. For instance, the human body's molecular makeup complete from head to toe. Portraying a scenario of similar possibilities, a tornado goes through a junkyard or scrapyard, creating a full 747 jumbo jet.

Now shall we portray a scenario? If our solar system, our sun, and nine planets were created within a 24-hour clock. Earth was created in the last one hour: Man was created in the previous 10 seconds. Time-traveling from our solar system into the Milky Way galaxy and that is unknown Universe. And of interest, our earth is spinning at 1000 mph every 24 hours is one full day. Our moon goes around our planet every 30 days. Our earth and our moon travel at the speed of 66,000 mph traveling around the sun every 365 days. The light that comes from the North Star, as we see it, left the North Star 321 light-years ago, speed traveling at 186,000 mi/s, is impressive in itself. Perfect gravity. The gravity is in harmony with our molecular structure. Our gravity is in harmony throughout this whole Universe. It is perfect.

Now we have a bubble of oxygen around us, and we look with our Hubble telescope's as far out into the Universe beyond our comprehension or imagination, and we derived a word called infinity. The brevity of life in the Bible is a twinkle of an eye.

As compared to eternity, 1 million years from now, we will either be in heaven or hell. Evolution? Once again, the harmony and order could not have evolved this correctly without a master design.

Anyway, the miracles keep on coming. What mystifies personal experience and imagination is how blind many hundreds of thousands walk around unaware of this majestic creation. Matthew 7: 13. *Enter in at the strait gate: for wide is the gate, and broad is the way, leading to destruction, and many there be which go in there at.*

Keeping God first, saying prayers devoting life to God, and service are helping others get to the gates of heaven. Not for profit or prestige with spiritual discernment proceeds donated. God's gift to us his life. What we do with his life is our gift to God.

Keeping it simple, it is the year 2021, the year of our Lord Jesus Christ. There is so much prophecy leading up to the birth of Jesus Christ our Lord that is God coming down to this earth in the flesh. The word of God was written by about approximately 40 authors of all Jewish descendent in the Holy Spirit, working through them to write the word that is not disputed. And if we read Psalms 22, written 1000 years before the birth of Christ and detailed Jesus Christ our Lord coming to this earth and paying for our sins. Isaiah chapter 53, written 700 years before the birth of Christ, in detail explains the birth and death of Jesus Christ our Lord.

God only mentions this once in the Bible. John chapter 15: 13 – *there is no greater love than this, that one should lay down their life for their friend or neighbor.* This is the unconditional love that one would give their life for their friend.

An Eternal Gift Through God's Grace, Inspired to store my riches in heaven having nothing of worldly gratification.

And I thank God from heaven above for the Souls I genuinely love. We will be together again one day but not yet.

II Corinthians 5: 8: "*To be absent from the flesh, is to be present with the Lord.*"

John 14:27, "*I am leaving you with a gift-peace of mind and heart. And the peace I give is a gift the world cannot provide. So don't be troubled or afraid.* " Matthew 23: 14 – *woe unto you, scribes and Pharisees, hypocrites! For you, devour widows houses, and for a pretense make more extended prayer: therefore, you shall receive the greater damnation.*

Isaiah 10: 2 –. *To turn aside the needy from judgment, and to take away the right from the poor of my people, that widows may be there pray, and that they may rob the fatherless!* Jeremiah 49: 11 – *leave the orphan children, I will preserve them alive, and let the widows trust in me, says the Lord.* Psalms 68: 5 – *a father of the fatherless and the widows' judge is God in his holy habitation.* There is no higher honor in the Bible for the care of widows, orphans, disabled cared for with reverence from God and his amazing Grace.

And God has each star named, and he knows the number of hairs on our head. This love is so far beyond our comprehension: it's a love that flows that has no end is more in-depth than all the oceans. Stretches from sky to sky as far as the eye can see, and it just flows through us that the Holy Spirit Jesus Christ our Lord left with us from God our Holy Father. Jesus Christ went to the cross and shed his precious blood for our wretched sins. And God, our heavenly Father, created all of this for the love he has for his children. The abundance of harmony and order could not have evolved. Jesus Christ, our Lord, leaves us with the Holy Spirit that moves throughout the earth, answering our prayers and through us to help one another. And this is God's love.

And then shall we travel into our infinite unknown Universe beyond our wildest comprehension or imagination. How long are we here? If I were a diehard atheist, agnostic, secular humanist, anti-Semitism, and did not believe in God. The inspiration of the 6-foot hole awaiting at the end of this journey would be depression compared to eternal life.

Having Faith and knowing as a child of God, we have a soul. One million years from now, the decision is yours by the choices you make here. And the brevity of time is but a twinkle of an eye. The Bible can be summed up: if you do good things, good things will happen: if you do bad things, bad things will happen. Do more for others than you do for yourself. Our destiny or infinity Heaven or Hell?

CHAPTER 8

Ginette and Thomas's Romantic Introduction

Romantic communications, between Thomas and Ginette. Through emails and attachments, Yahoo messenger, telephone calls, and continuously developing this deep love, through God's grace.

Gorgeous please, try exercising loving kindness to yourself through the grace of God and the Holy Spirit. Be nice to yourself because you worth it, and I'm very proud of you. No worry no stress or pressure that is a moment of happiness you will never get back. Everything is okay right this very moment, the last minute is gone and the next minute is not here yet.

No resentments no regrets, we cannot turn the clock back and go back in time. All we can do sweetheart together is move forward to make this a better world for those precious souls out there. And please do not take yourself too seriously, God does have a sense of humor.

Although I do not feel I know this lady entirely, she lives a life rightfully, free, and brings joy to others.

In the part of your life, that is not my business, and even if it were mine. This companion may not make you happy. You knew this before I did.

This is how I learned from you, and you may not understand why I say the things I do? If I were not writing to you right now and thinking about you.

Even if you feel it is the wrong thing to say or write, I am learning through the Holy Spirit, looking back at what I have written to you. That many things were wrong, I will be the first to admit that, and that's how I learn: I learn not to do that again.

Especially, why would I do that to the one that God sent me, and the one I am supposed to provide for and love unconditionally, and that's you? Will never want for anything, that is, God's will not mine, and in my heart spiritually, I know that God will provide for us extensively with Grace.

God does not have two precious souls, such as ours, come together without delivering, with Faith, prayers, and love for God. Peace and elegance of the Lord, be with you and your mother, through Jesus Christ, our Lord's name, amen.

February 2018 Year Of Our Lord Romantic Memoirs From Heaven

On Thursday, February 15, 2018,

Ginette wrote:

It's excellent to hear from you here soon, and I appreciate you for sharing your email address with me. I will know more about you if you do not mind telling me. I am Ginette here, single. I am a true believer and pray to meet someone who shares the same faith with me here. Till I can hear from you soon. In Christ, Ginette.

On Thursday, February 15, 2018,

Thomas wrote :

> *We are both Christians: we believe in the same thing. I read the Bible daily and write Christian books about miracles. My email address you have, may I ask where you live? That could be the deciding factor, and God blessed with love and prayers, Thomas. Clean as well as my home. I love to laugh and have fun, and I'm a very kind, caring, generous, and romantic landline telephone number.*
>
> *Thank you very much for responding, and I appreciate you asking, and we will see where God takes us. God bless with love and prayers, Thomas.*

Ginette wrote:

> *Hello Thomas,*
>
> *Glad to hear from you soon, You're more welcome, and it's my pleasure we both are a chance to talk on here. How are you doing? I hope you're doing great. I am fine here, and I believe that we both will get to know each other much better with constant communication. I am sometimes on Yahoo messenger. If you have an idea about it, we can chat from there. I did add your email address already. May God take both of us through each day and let us keep the light of Christ brighten in the darkness, that through our life in the dark many will see and get salvation as well. Let us talk more. Till again. In Christ. Ginette.*

Thomas wrote:

Thank you, Ginette. I Love you. God loves you when you get to Arizona, and please look me up. I will have a spare bedroom.

Ginette wrote:

Hello Thomas,

It's a pleasure hearing from you once again. I'm sorry I didn't reply right away. Oh yes, it would be okay to finally meet you in person because that's my wish to be with someone that can indeed have a sweet life together. My focus right now is getting to know you much better. I know in so doing, it's not a one-day thing. It's a process.

I want to ask a few questions as I see this way I get to know you better, so I hope you don't mind asking. Lol. First: How long have you lived in Arizona? Where are you initially from? Do you have relatives like brothers and sisters or your parents? I mean, if anyhow close are you to them? Are you interested in having kids? Do you still have intentions of getting married? How serious are you in getting into any relationship, or do you want a friend? I will ask more next time, and please forgive my many questions lol it's the only way I think I'll know you better. Feel free to ask me anything, and I'll be more than willing to answer you. Have a beautiful day until I hear from you again — your Ginette.

Thomas wrote:

Ginette I'm going to write to you later. I'm on the telephone now, thank you, love you. Write to me please: I love you and miss you and love talking to you: I have time now. Love you the way you like to be loved, pray you to love to be loved the way I would love you. God bless with God's love and speed, that we get to see one another soon.

Ginette wrote:

Hello Thomas,

How sweet to hear from you! I'm glad to be able to hear from you once again: I hope you're having a lovely time. Well, thanks for expressing your heart to me that you love me. I think I have some liking for you, but I would like to know you more and be sure we are meant for one another. You seem a nice person, and I have an interest in learning from you much better.

It has been cold here, and not much has been going on recently.

I like to ask you a few more questions, and I hope you don't have any problem with me asking you: I only want to know you each day.

I like to know the most important things you are looking for in another partner? What are some of your interests? What have past relationships taught you? Do you drink or smoke? What do you think about affairs?

I look forward to hearing from you soon, and thanks so much for your message again. May you have a blessed day.

My regards. Ginette

Thomas wrote:

Thank you very much for responding. I apologize for not getting back to you sooner. The most crucial thing in a relationship is that the lady is a Christian, believes in God, Jesus Christ, the Bible, the saints, the Angels, the prophets, and everything that has to do with Christianity. I read the Bible daily. Although I am not perfect, I am an ordained minister, cannot walk on water, and I do not believe you can either.

So we each have our character defects, and we each have our spiritual gifts: I do not drink or do drugs in the last four years, and I have no intentions of doing them ever again. I pray to God, He lifted the mental obsession and the physical compulsion, helping others recover from alcohol and drugs.

I smoke cigarettes very seldom, very little: I smoke American spirit yellows, usually take 2 to 3 drags off a cigarette, and put it out, and I will not smoke around a lady that does not burn. Now I have a few lady friends, they can trust me, communicate, and have a conversation is essential to me I miss not holding and hugging a lady.

Ginette wrote:

Hello Thomas, I'm so glad to hear from you, and it is so fantastic hearing from you sooner, do not apologize for not being on time: you're beautiful. I know things come up some times, I wish always to hear from you, and I like to continue to remember you bit by bit, you seem a nice person really to admit.

I agree with you, and I think being in Christ or having someone that shares the same faith is essential: being like-minded has its positive aspect. I'm a spirit-filled person, and Christ is my foundation since I received Christ. My life has changed so much. My understanding of life and religion has also changed, so meeting someone like you a blessing to me, one that I grow together. I believe real true love is the one that is in Christ because when two honest and Christ-loving persons are in love, there's nothing to separates the two hearts joined together by Christ.

I'm glad that you don't smoke like you used to do, it is sad what drug has done to many people's lives, but when one is lucky to be saved, I think that person is very blessed. I don't smoke and would never have a problem with someone who does that: as long as that person is decent, I shouldn't complain.

I'm so sorry that you have lived alone for so long: I can imagine what it takes to live all by oneself: you sound like a good man, I have been alone for a while, and I do not like it already, so I truly understand, I think without you and me can have a life full of happiness. Still, sometimes things do not happen overnight, and you must pray of whom God is directing you: let's continue to keep in touch, and with God above, we can see what is in store for us.

I will like to ask you a few questions, and you feel free to ask me well, and I will be more than happy to do so.

Besides love, what one trait have you noticed in couples that have maintained a successful relationship for many years? Describe an interest you have that you would honestly hope your partner could share with you? How will your perfect day? If you had any wishes, what would they be? What are your most outstanding achievements? I wish you a blessed day, and I'm looking forward to hearing from you. My best regards to you.

Your Ginette.

Thomas wrote:

Ginette, thank you very much: I will start with your questions. I do not notice other people's relationships that have to maintain success: there is always a flipside to the coin. I have known people married 50 years plus. They were the most unhappy people: I feel God in Jesus Christ and faith in communication and open communication and truth with trust.

God is the key in Jesus Christ's name, those who pray to stay together.

I would pray that my partner shared everything with me that would be honesty and trust, a perfect day for me is turning my will and my life care of God and devoting my life to God and service: my most outstanding achievement is having faith in God through Jesus Christ our Lord's name,

I will pray for you because I care about you. I pray we are honest with one another and can develop a friendship that will last, and eternal friendship we do not get married for death do us apart we get married until we reunited in heaven, God bless with love and prayers your friend (Soul mate?) call me if you get the opportunity or give me your telephone number. I will contact you if you agree.

Ginette wrote:

Good morning, Thomas: it's fantastic hearing from you and having the time to sit to write you back. I am always happy to do so, and I can see we are getting along day by day: all is patience, and a lasting friendship comes with the patient, when one realizes the trust that exists between two people, it's how more profound people get so I understand what you say, and that's the truth.

God controls everything in life, so I like how you turn almost every aspect of your life to Christ, and I like that: there's something to learn from you and know that though we want a friendship or maybe more, I want to learn many things from you too.

Like I said, whatever in life, be it a friendship or relationship without certain qualities, people would just be wasting precious time, these are what you mentioned, honesty and trust. Thanks so much for taking the time to answer my questions. I so appreciate that. Please feel free to ask me, and I promise to tell you what you like to know: I want to know you more and more, it's one reason I ask questions, so I'll do it again.

Are you a jealous type? How much of their spare time should your partner spend with you? What does growing old mean to you? What do others admire about you?

Thanks so much for taking the time to write to me, and I look to hearing from you soon. Have a blessed day until I hear from you again. My warm regards to you — your Ginette.

Thomas wrote:

God bless in Jesus Christ, our Lord's name.

Ginette wrote:

Hello Thomas,

It's nice to hear from you, and I'm happy about the coming up of your new book. I will check the Amazon and see. How's your day going? I hope all is going well with you. My day is going well, and I will be going out later for a few errands, but I thought to write to you first. It is so unique each time I hear from you. What are your plans for today?

I look to hearing from you again, and you have a blessed day. I am praying and thinking about you. My regards, Ginette.

Thomas wrote:

Why do we always have to have a plan? My plan would be for a nice Christian lady such as yourself to come to our home where we can have fun and laugh as kindred spirits.

MARCH 2018, ROMANTIC MEMOIRS FROM HEAVEN

Ginette wrote:

Hey, Thomas, You make me smile, and I do agree with you! I hope you're having a lovely Sunday. Mine is going great as well. It's any reasonable person's dream to have a particular person in his or her life to be happy. I would think the same about you, too, to have you knocking on my door someday. Would you like that? Anyway, I wanted to ask you if you don't mind chatting on Yahoo messenger, this way we could hear from each other on time. Just let me know, and I will add you there. We will sometimes text on the phone if you like that as well. I'll also give you a call soon, and I feel nervous, especially the first time, lol. Have a beautiful day. I look to hearing from you soon. My regards. Ginette.

Thomas wrote:

Ginette, Christian, and that's the kind of lady I'm looking for, my priority those who pray together stay together. One moment of worry is a moment of happiness we will never get back. I love to laugh and have fun, especially making other people laugh my mind off the trials and tribulations. God loves you, and for that, I love you for who you are. And I appreciate your time, your great lady. I have a lot to do, sweetheart, today. I will keep in touch with you, and okay, God bless with love and prayers, Thomas.

Ginette wrote:

Good morning Thomas, You seem like a romantic guy, and I can imagine how much it would be interesting having a life with you: in doing so, I believe I must trust you and know that you're someone that respect a lady.

I want a guy in my life that would make me feel special every day and, in return, love him with all my heart. I think you'll be that person and I look to knowing you much better. I know it's a process. Still, with the both of us attracted to each other we can have a happy life of quality love, romance and I promise to be for only you but I must know you're the right person and not just for saying it but being that person I can count on, one I can show my Mom and friends.

I added you on Yahoo messenger, so try to accept my request there, and we can chat there. You make me feel so happy, and I look to being close. Have a beautiful day, and I look forward to hearing from you and chatting. My regards to you. Ginette.

I'm so excited to hear from you once again. I hope your weekend is going great! Mine is busy as I'm doing some cleaning and washing. I got lazy and decided to write to you: instead, you have been on my mind so much. And I am falling for you so much with so many romantic words.

It is sad when some ladies put materials first instead of the importance of a good relationship. And there is so much love you have to offer than material things: I believe as long you love and respect your partner, the rest will follow, sad that you have been alone so long. You sound like a good guy, and my heart tells me you're, I have been talking to my Mom about you for a while now, and she thinks you're going to be the right person to me and advise me to love and respect you. It's my dream to have a caring partner who respects his woman, would make her feel like a queen, a man that will make me feel special each time, one that I will make my king as well.

Your true love is vital in any healthy relationship, and I don't mind the romantic lady wants, so having you with such would make my world. The best part of a relationship to satisfy a lady is material things and what happens in the bedroom. I want a man I will need each time I feel loving and promise to satisfy when he feels love. It's not fair to deny good guy love when he needs it, but that guy must be understanding as well not to treat his wife like an animal.

I love hearing from you so much Thomas, I'm here thinking about you, and all the right time, we will share can't wait to be with you someday. I must get back to cleaning, and you have a lovely weekend. I included a pic for you and hope you'll like it. Warm regards. Your Ginette.

Thomas wrote:

Ginette,

I pray you are doing well today: my prayers are with you and thank you very much for the picture. You're a charming young lady. It still concerns me that our age difference may be a factor, now please forgive me. I forget what country you come from, Uganda? Have you checked on what it would take for you to get to the United States?

I keep looking at your picture, and you are so beautiful and young.

I would not deprive you of anything. I'm not a jealous man or a controlling man, and I would not tell you what to do unless you as. I have learned a lot throughout my life and especially how to treat a lady I would care about and love. It is tough to get into the United States with our president at this point. That is why I ask you if you could check on what it would take for you to get to the United States. As I have mentioned before, to keep loving, you must let it go, and if you wanted to do things with other men that I could not do, that would be okay for the simple reason, I do not wish to deprive you of life. As long as you know, and we both know that your heart belongs to me, and my heart belongs to you.

I would want to get married as soon as possible I'm not too comfortable with fornication or adultery, and as beautiful as you are, I realize that you must have had a boyfriend in the past. I do have lady friends that I communicate with, and I wouldn't say I like the way men treat ladies: for the most part, a man would tell you anything he thinks you want to hear to get into your pants if you know what I mean. And if that were your choice to be with someone else other than myself, I would pray for you and wish you the best. God bless with love and prayers, Thomas.

Ginette wrote:

Hey Thomas,

It's so amazing hearing from you once again. I'm glad you like my pic, and thanks for the compliment. I so appreciate your prayers each time. Know that you're always in mine. Well, I have also been thinking about the age difference between us, but then I can't judge love. Love knows no age or boundaries. After all, age is just a number: as long a person can give you the desired tenderness, it does not matter how old they're. As I told you before, I have had a boyfriend, my high school boyfriend who I loved so much: we were both young people, and what I got from him was a complete mess and was like living in hell, there is where my judgment got changed that true love isn't the age but the heart of a person towards you.

Oh, you forgot which country? I thought you remember, I'm from Canada, my Dad is originally from Malta, an island near Italy, but I haven't been there before. Well, I have thought about traveling, but I have not decided yet where my Mom has been planning to go to Malta with me to visit my Dad's native home. I have also plan to visit the United States, so let us see what's happening.

That's very sad what you went through with women. No wonder you said some ladies are not the best, but I won't defend all of them. Still, there would always be those with good hearts, and I think it is dumb for someone to put money first in a relationship. Consider the most critical thing in any relationship: love, thinking good about the person you want to love, and treating them the same way you would like. You weren't a bad or weak person: those that took advantage of you didn't know what it takes for someone to care for another.

Yes, I realize you have somewhat been skeptical, but I won't judge you. You have the right to do so if you have had a bad experience with a dishonest person or people. I can't blow my own trumpet, but my character must show my image. No one knows what may happen the next minute though, for me, what I'm looking for is a caring person, affectionate type of guy. To experience the love I have never experienced before, not having someone that will abuse me and take me less, as long I can have love and respect from a guy, I too would give the same back in return.

I don't look too much at the physical appearance of a person, but mainly their heart, the heart a person has towards you is more than anything else in life, you're a nice-looking person and handsome too to admit,

God made you unique in His image, and you are as important as anyone. I agree: most people would expect a young lady to love the outdoors, but then what we get from the outdoor activities? Just pleasure, hiking, dancing, the nightlife is to satisfy the flesh, but the most important part is love, all the things you named that you can do with your body are already what every average person would do so I some see you as a handicap you're as unique as me. I appreciate your understanding spirit, and another thing is I realize you genuinely respect the views of others and respect a lady: that's what I look like in a man, and you have so many good qualities that you may not know.

Still, then every country has its value, and each individual has what it takes to develop. Many states have opportunities that the US does not have here in Canada, and it is more peaceful and less crime rate compared to the US and other countries. The US is unique in its ways, though. When the time comes as long, we want to live together to love and care for each other, and a way must be there no matter what Trump does. All we need is to pray and continue to love each other.

Of course, I want to get married too! So it is right now to have someone and have kids and be established. I wouldn't be like other girls fooling themselves, thinking that age is still in their favor. That's hazardous thinking for a lady. Yes, I had a boyfriend, but he was a beast. He beat on me and made me feel uncomfortable, but we finally went our way. I think you and I are getting along well, and I'm sure with God, nothing is impossible.

I understand what you mean, and men are very good at that to be like saints from the beginning, but as soon as they know all about you, they become different people, you know so much of what women go through, and my heart is already falling for you.

I have been talking much about you to my Mom and showed her your picture and messages, the very recent ones though not from the start, and she thinks you're looking for the same thing. I'm also looking for, so I must continue to correspond with you and put everything in my prayers.

She said you're an honest heart looking for a like-minded person. She encourages me not to look at age but as a character. So who knows, we must be lucky! Thanks so much for the charming message, and you have a blessed Sunday. My heart goes to you—your Ginette.

Thomas wrote:

Ginette, everything your time and compassion and kindness, I feel you're the spirit God will put in our lives. I certainly enjoyed reading your letter and getting to know you as a friend that would devote their lives to God and serve.

You have a decision to make sounds similar, although not the same as other ladies I have communicated with, it seems they always have to go to another country to see some relatives such as their father. The bottom line is all they want is money. I have a strong feeling you are not one of those ladies, and coming from Canada to the United States, and I do not believe that difficult.

You're the first lady who looked at my heart, and we are only here a short time to learn our lessons go through our trials and tribulations, and help as many people as we can get to heaven for eternity. Life here on this earth is but a blink of an eye, I will never lie to you, and we will grow together in love, a God-given gift of grace that it appeared to me we both deserve.

Romans 3:4 God forbid: yea, let God be true, but every man a liar: as it is written, That thou mightest be justified in thy sayings, and mightiest overcome when thou art judged.

I will have to admit honestly, and you're the very first lady that has ever written to me the way you have. I have a good feeling spiritually that we will grow together in love through the grace of God and continue to be happy, joyous, and free. I feel what you had to say is from your heart, and like you had mentioned, I expect the same from you as you would for me. I know your mother did not take that picture of you. Did you take the picture??

I keep looking at it and praying to God that you are the lady and Soulmate that God will put into my life. God willing, you speak the truth. It would seem to me that it. It would not make my work Canadian citizen come to the United States. It will be a miracle if a biblical proportion of everything you have written to me is honest and sincere. Not one omen out to God shall go unpaid, and I pray for instant karma, and I get it because at the end of the journey, I know I'm going straight to heaven: my faith is unshakable.

I pray you do not mind breaking anonymity. I show your picture to a lady friend of mine and praying your not another scammer. I do not tell anyone about our conversation between one another, between God and yourself and me. And I know my faith is so incapable of being unshakable. I have enough experience, and you are a very young lady, whispered through discernment. I admire and would carry us into heaven through the grace of God, and God willing, you are what I pray for and have been praying for years.

It's almost like Christmas morning, and there is no such thing as luck. Everything happens for a reason. Through the Holy Spirit, we pray that answered our prayers are moving throughout the earth. Also, have you checked on what it would take for you to come into the United States? Since the United States and Canada are close allies in my mind's eye, it cannot be that hard? Or difficult. There's so much that we have to learn about one another, love Thomas.

Ginette wrote:

Hello Thomas, Sorry I didn't get back to you right away. It was so lovely to hear from you once again. How are you doing today? I hope your day is going well, so far mine started not too long ago, so I look to the rest of the day. It makes me happy to hear that you enjoy reading my messages: I also do yours.

You're right: we all maybe ladies but do not have the same characters or same thoughts of the mind: people think differently. It is not a bad idea for a person to ask but do that honestly, too, I do not like dishonest people, and I have had issues with a few people trusting them. Yes, that's right, I don't think the process or documents one needs from Canada to the US is the same as other North American countries. We will see what happens as we get along.

Well, you're right: I look mainly at someone's heart position.

I do not go judging people while not knowing what may be going on in their hearts. Since we started corresponding, I have always known you were someone in the same position as me, looking for an honest heart. I, too, have prayed a long time for a like-minded person for me. I do not just jump in making decisions without first praying about things, I have been doing that, and my heart accepts you. Without a doubt, the two spirits are going along well, so I know God is up to something good: it is only possible when both of us accept His plan for our lives. I agree the Bible say what profits a man when he gains the whole world and loses his soul? It's a mere question but a very touching one too: if many people thought this question, I don't think people will go their thoughts, this question is supposed to bring each person to the realization that everyone is as important as oneself. The actual subject of Jesus Christ to this world was to love, love, and love one another because humans do not share such feelings. That's why Christ always told people to do so. If we love one another, no one would want to hurt another.

After all, not everyone understands the true meaning of love: that's why people do what they do, reasons those ladies you met treated you the way they did, but they say you never know the best until you finally have it.

You must be a kind heart that wants to help others in trouble: the best a child of God can do is bringing the lost souls over to the kingdom of God, and that's what you're doing. Let me share one confession with you since I got saved, and I always see myself talking about God even though I do not feel relaxed in my self. Still, as I hate to do so, the more I see myself sharing about God during conversations, even those who do not have anything to do with the gospel. I feel I'm a young girl who wants to live to the fullest, but God is always interrupting. Lol,

No, that pic wasn't my Mom. It was a friend: I stay with a friend in the apartment we rented due to my Mom's house's distance from my workplace: I go over during the weekend to see my Mom. My Mom would never want to take such a picture for me. I only asked my friend to take that picture since you were naughty.

I see your doubt, and I didn't know you would have issues with the picture I sent you. I didn't see the content of the image would become a problem. Honestly, I felt the way you sounded romantic in your letters. I would do the same. I think your female friend is the one that put more doubts in your heart about my picture, and I hate when people judge others because of their dress. I am saved but do not cut myself from wearing fashionable clothing: that's where many who claim to be Christians missed the mark, the judge so much from others' outward appearances. I hope you're not the same type of person Thomas. I believe if you did share our conversations with that lady female of yours, she wouldn't have judged me in the way she did.

As I said, I don't try to prove anything to anyone. I rather God be my judge, not man, so I leave it with you how you feel about me, not what another thinks about me. I will continue to depend on the Lord for direction, and I know what is meant cannot be changed.

I haven't checked on the process of coming to the US yet, and I will do that as we get along: I'll check as soon as I have some time and update you. It would be my joy to be with a person who genuinely loves me, starts a life together, and sees what God brings into our lives. As long God is in our meeting and has a plan for us, nothing would be too complicated. I continue to think about you and hope you do the same for me also. I look to knowing one another each day, and so far, I have the faith that we meant for one another. We believe that God can do the impossible. I understand what you say: it is God that gives children. I know He wants me to have some, and if it is you, He must make you do that, nothing too hard to God, so we shouldn't doubt anything.

I hope you will have a good day, and I look to hearing from you soon. You're always on my heart. Never forget that. Warmest regards to you, From your secret admirer Ginette.

Thomas wrote:

Ginette, I missed your email, and I miss you not being able to email me, thank you very much: I appreciate your time reading your emails makes my heart warm and spiritually more connected to you.

I realize that the time spent writing to me tells me a lot about you, that you do care. I'm getting more of a spiritual connection with you and drawn to you more each day. You are a great lady, and I like you a lot. God loves you. I do think about you every day I look at your picture, you're so young and beautiful, do you think it would be fair if we were to share a life?

You have so much experience to live, and I would not for the life of me want to keep you back from living that life to the fullest. As I had mentioned before, I'm not a jealous or controlling man and very kindhearted, and I have great compassion for ladies. Therefore, I feel ladies are more intelligent than men, which I adore about you. Is that you're so young and drawn to a man such as myself, we can teach each other the love we have never known.

I love to laugh and have fun as we will when we get together, God willing. Trust and honesty and the love of God in Jesus Christ our Lord's name as Christians. I would enjoy your companionship, communication, and company, and I would love to love you the way you like to be loved. I would enjoy just touching you and giving you a gentle massage, a very sensual massage slowly and softly.

As long as we would enjoy each other's love for one another and try different things consensually and grow in love together. I am a good lover, and I have had a lot of experience, never with the right Christian lady. And that area will have to grow in our love for one another, and it will be so precious that we can know love together and bond with God.

You would love the way I love you, and I would like the way you love me: If you have any more photos, please send them: I would appreciate that. I have a spiritual feeling we will be together one day, growing in love and helping others to set an example of how life should live between two people. Because of the letters you write to me, I feel a secure spiritual connection: one thing you do have that other ladies do not have is the time to write to me and let me know your feelings.

I will never lie to you, and I'll never cheat on you or even think of it, primarily your heart. I would protect that, and we would grow together with passion and desire. I would love nothing better than to be together with you right now, and I would love you so nicely. Together, we will go along and love one another, the cherry on the cake, and I would like to love you.

You would love to be loved by me and teach me. I pray I am not offending you, I would protect you, and we would have fun together growing in love together. I cannot stop looking at that picture: you turn me on so much, so I'm going to leave for now because I'm thinking about us: I would love to love you.

The precious beautiful young lady I will love one day and when our heart is bonded with each other and growing in strength. I would want you to do things to live out your life that I cannot do. I will not hold you back because you're worth it: you're so precious. I just want to kiss you very slowly.

So I will leave, for now, sweetheart, you dear beautiful, tasty, lovely lady. Tell me how you will love me, what you like me to do to you, what you would like to grow together, and our love for one another sensually.

A friend of mine, said is his wife was not happy with him so he left. I said really? And I asked my friend, how did she take that? He said, "You know, you live with someone for 20 years, and you think you know them. I did not realize my wife could sing and do cartwheels at the same time.

I just pray that we do not have to look back on this scenario and feel that we are getting tired of each other. On the significant other is boring, and does not show any interest in the relationship or marriage. Let us together remember this love from God and always remember our calling together. And how we came together through the grace of God. We would be creating the greatest injustice against ourselves and our souls.

I would love to take care of you preciously and protect you. We will live with each other with the desire that two soul mates met, enjoying one another. I'm going to have a good day, beautiful, my precious soul mate sweetheart, oh how I love you, and God bless with love and prayers your Soul mate Thomas.

Ginette wrote:

I just got done reading your lengthy message, and all the romantic things said, you're just my kind of man to admit, you sound young at heart, and I can't resist you!

How are you doing? I hope you're doing great and safe. By the Lord's grace, I'm fine and thank Him for the opportunity given us to grow together.

I am always on the lookout waiting on your messages, and whenever I hear from you, I am so excited. Good that you thought about our privacy: I have no problem with you telling people about us or our happiness. But then some people are so fast in sticking their noses in other people's affairs sometimes, not because they care, but to know about your personal life.

If you face an unfortunate situation, they laugh at your back, and most women do that: that's why I felt somehow said about the judgment your lady friend tried to judge me on. Even my girlfriend, who lives with me here, is not all we tell each other: we have our limit. I also feel we are connected spiritually and are mature enough to control our destiny. I am getting to pour my trust in you, and I do not want any interruption: I hope you feel the same as well.

Well, I don't think it is unfair to love someone older, as long as that person understands why there would be an issue with loving them. Once you are an honest heart who wants a lady to be happy and that lady also enjoys the same things, I believe they should be relevant to each other. I have been in a relationship with a young person like myself before. I saw hell and trying an older person who can treat me better than my previous relationship, and then no need not be happy or scary.

One person I look up to as my role model is Celine Dion, she did marry an older man, and they loved each other till the end, so the same can go for you and me, only I want you to live longer so we can enjoy each other..lol I need you to live another more 50 years. Lol,

It amazes me that you are such a kind person, one that is not controlling: one thing most men miss out that they want to control. In doing that, ladies look for ways to trick them, as long you are free in the heart and trust a lady. She can have the conscious and, in return, love you and treats you sound like a man. It's like having a child with you and you as a parent being so harsh on the child, and it makes a child get Incorrigible. Then just being cool, hoping to see if they have the will power to be useful, not necessarily having to take a rod, such a child become the right person naturally: it's the same with women.

With all you mentioned to admit and hoping it's only you and me. I want you so much, causes me to want to love you more because the difference between an older man and a young man is that, so if my man got the same, why wish to think about someone younger. You're just so sweet and amazes me. I would want to hold you tight and scream in your name several times because you make me think, lovey. I will give you myself, you can have me all to yourself and we enough quality love. All I'm hoping is to not go against my faith: as long everything is on the right path, there's nothing I can't do for you. I know you're going to be my man, and me, your wife. I have included a picture for you.

I am thinking so much about you today. Be safe, and I look forward to hearing from you. I wanted to tell you to sign in to your Yahoo messenger since we both have the app. I did message you there.

Yours sincerely, Ginette.

Thomas wrote:

I always look forward to your letters as well, the key to love his trust. You know you're in love when the hardest thing to do is say goodbye. If you love someone, tell them because hearts often are broken by words left unspoken. Alter your attitude, and you can alter your life. I pray for my soul, with love, that forgiveness is God's will. I am the light: he who follows me will never be in darkness. I love you, Jesus Christ.

Ephesians 3:20, concentrate on the first sentence. "The will of God will never take you, where the grace of God will not protect you." Something good will happen to you today. Something that you have been waiting to hear. That is my prayer for you today.

I never thought that God could or would work in our lives: those who pray together stay together. I'm a Christian, and only through the grace of God I am blessed.

Perfection is the set up for disappointment. It is not the Garden of Eden, and everything happens for a reason: giving and receiving is a two-way street.

I am attending the third funeral of good friends within the last few months, and I am still behind the eight ball with God, not finished with me yet. We must always remain faithful and trust one another with faith in God, pray together, we will stay together. I store my riches in heaven. Matthew6: 20 - 21, "store up riches in heaven for your heart will always be. Where your riches are."

Sometimes I feel that my Soul mate, In heaven, you are waiting for me. I refuse to have a detrimental second, I thoroughly insist on enjoying life, and I do not take myself too seriously. I try not to let people, places, or things, including myself, rent space in my head. No drama, God has me right where I need to be.

In my eyes, my Soul mate (yourself) is the only woman in the world. Honor yourself when you hold yourself high with integrity and self-respect, and never compromise your values: you can trust each other. It is the basis for everything else that defined your life and your marriage. Honor each other, do not hesitate to see — more in each other than what is present at face value.

Look deep, and people tend to live up to our expectations of them.

I found these inserts that the Holy Spirit is working through me and only through the grace of God in Jesus Christ, our Lord. I look forward to your emails, you are a beautiful young lady, and I pray to God with my physical limitations that it would not be selfish of me to get into a relationship with the lovely young lady that has a life in front of her. I am praying to God about this: thank you very much for the picture: you are a sweetheart. And I love how you love me, and I'm going to love you. With the knowledge and wisdom of my past mistakes, you are a knowledgeable and intuitive lady.

I am going to tickle you when I see you, smile, and we are going to laugh together and have fun together. And after we build this cake, we will put the cherry on the top, and it will be a never-ending process between the two of us.

We will love each other and grow together for the simple reason we will have a life of love for God and grow together spiritually. Because you are worth it, and I care. I am just thinking about you and looking at your pictures, and I can satisfy your needs and anytime. Consensually we will have a passion for one another and with our unshakable faith. God will take care of us of the love and trust we have in one another. I think I'm starting to like you, smile, and I might be falling in love with you.

Your thoughts with reassuring trust that supports spirit and faith. — understanding the ability to comprehend not only the unspoken word but these unspoken gestures, the little things that may not be too much by themselves.

Love is a friendship that has caught fire. It is quiet understanding, confidence, sharing, and forgiving loyalty through formal and inconvenient times. It settles for nothing less them perfection and makes allowances for human weaknesses. Love is content with the present, hope for the future, and it does not brood over the past.

It is a day in, day out, a chronicle of irritations, problems, compromises, small disappointments, significant victories, and working toward a common goal.

If you have love in your life, it can make up for many things you lack. God blessed with love and prayers, Thomas,

I wish you were here so I could be with you and love you. I think about you more often than you may realize. You are precious, and I know I will encourage you to live your life knowing that your heart belongs to me: how could I deprive you of the experience? What am I going to say to God when I get to heaven? My prophecy prediction is that Jesus Christ is coming, I know not when, Jesus comes like a thief in the night.

Ginette wrote:

Hey Thomas!

I got your message yesterday and thought to reply today since I was busy. It makes me so happy to hear from you each day. I hope you're having a beautiful day: mine is going slow here and quiet but writing back to you makes it better for me.

I agree love cannot go without trust: the two go in parallel, saying goodbye sometimes in a relationship can be sad and cannot be sad depending on the situation. When leaving a bad relationship, you do not get that tragic, and it is when you cherished and love that person that goodbyes become a burden.

You're right: loving another person is the best one can do: life is too short to be alone, so when you meet someone deserving, it is good to hold that person tight and don't let them go. It's the situation that we are in right now, letting me go and not letting you go because the two spirits are flowing so smoothly. Sure, when we follow Jesus Christ, we are never in darkness: we get into the light, no one in the morning would have a sad life: the view is a total joy. Wow, how sweet you are dear, the sentence is so touching!

I wish many people knew this, that the will of God would not take you where the grace of God cannot protect you: you are so right, I can feel it, and I have experienced it in my life. When I fell in love with my high school boyfriend, it was my will. Still, I knew deep in my heart, it was God's will, and then though my intention took me into his life, the grace of God would not protect me, so the relationship failed! I'm a witness to this exact sentence you mentioned.

Well, yes, you never know what's next in life, and I never knew I would have fallen in love with someone older. I didn't believe that I would develop a feeling for an older person or having someone like you pouring out so much love. We called this destiny: I can see the real purpose of my life now. And what I thought wasn't God's plan for my life, I can feel the deep happiness in my heart since I met you, Thomas.

That is true: the six things you listed are from Proverbs' book are so real: these are common among people. And if you are not stable in the Lord, you would see yourself doing such: it would be the worst things to do what the Lord hates! From my perspective, if people ceased from all these things, life would have been so happy on earth.

I do not think you have any limitations that would be selfish to me: the saddest barrier that would stop me from loving you is when you do not like me. I do not look much at a person's physical look: I am mostly concerned with the heart and the inner part of a person. You are a unique person, and I appreciate you as you are. Pure enjoyment is when you have someone that pours out their heart to you. Good to hear that you love my picture, can you send me some of yours again? I did save the one you posted, and you are a fine gentleman more than you know.

I am thinking about you and hope your day is going great.

I am so proud of you to know that you love me, and with all the descriptions make me want to enjoy day to day, you are getting more rooted in my heart. And I can tell that we are just the best life can offer: I promise you to love you till the end and hope you will do the same. I will get busy now, and forgive me if

I leave out some things you expected me to say, just ask me, and I am willing to answer you anytime. You are so sweet, Thomas, and know I love you so much and want you so much. Have a beautiful day, and I look to hearing from you once again. You're my king!

Your Ginette

Thomas wrote:

Give me a few minutes, and please want to pray about this letter, and take my time. I need an answer from God, and I want to say the right things and be honest.

Please do not keep God out of the equation or our life: you and I both know that is why we are together forever and eternity: you are my girl. And I am, in love with you, well, I would not say, I am passionately in love with you. Things are going to get better, sweetheart. And Faith in God, it hurts my heart to know you're angry.

When you get the time, if it possible for you to, please call me, on the telephone, or give me a time when I can contact you on the phone? I want to talk to you. I would like to hear your beautiful sweet voice, for not just a minute or two, could we spend some time together on the telephone?

And it was just you and I, as one in spirit with such a calming piece of strength, that God was right there with us. I will never forget the feeling, and maybe you can help explain? Or perhaps you have experienced similar feelings?

And what I think about is when you said, "Do I love you"?

That stuck in my mind and is still there. I know I said some things that set you free from our commitment to one another. With no jealousy, with no control, with no ownership, and with the lost connection of God. That initially brought us together, and that was very selfish of me. You teach me so much about love that we will experience one day, and God is bringing me deeper into that love with you.

Please let me know, sweetheart, do you see a change in my love for you? From the time we have first met up until this point, time? We are yet, we are one, and we are three, with God in our lives together. With the spiritual love that could only have come from above.

And you were the Angel that was sent to me to initiate this love between us, and for that, I cannot explain this love I have for you, and us and, most importantly, for God, through Jesus Christ, our Lord's name.

I pray to God that you are happy in your room compared to the motel you are staying at: how are your accommodations? Do you like it? Are you happy? I have a feeling we will never be delighted until we are together: that is my feeling.

I keep having this reoccurring thought of you, and I lay in bed together holding each other, and it is a love and compassion I have never experienced with anyone.

I'm so looking forward to that day when we will be holding each other in bed — then looking at the big picture down the road. The one thing that hurts my heart is the financial difficulties we are going through right now.

It must be hard for you to be in love with a man that cannot provide for you financially. We have way too many things in common to say that our relationship happened perchance. It happened through the Grace of God, and why we are going through these financial difficulties together, only God knows.

We are a dream team, and the dreams and goals we have in front of us are so beautiful and breathtaking. God has brought you into my life, and you have been the glue that has continuously hung on. To our relationship, our marriage, and our love together, and this is why you are so unique in the eyes of God.

I look back on how I treated you and the things I said, and you still would not give that love up. As hard as it must've been for you at times, and still is, I'm sure. It has made me realize how precious you are and what a God-given gift you have been to me. I love you so much, sweetheart. I am in love with you so much.

I look forward to the day when we are finally a family.

Please do not ever feel frustrated or that I do not love you any less for not putting in the time that I can.I am fortunate and blessed to have a gorgeous lady such as yourself in my life. You are teaching me about love and holding onto that love with everything you have. And if I have said anything recently to have hurt your feelings or have not made you feel good about yourself.

Please do not hesitate to let me know because I am a man. You are a woman, and we are different in our God-given spiritual characteristics, yet it will be so beautiful and precious when we come together. I love you, my sweet Ginette: you are my girl, and please let your mother know that my prayers are with her. I care about her with reverence, and she will be so blessed with the most precious gift of her grandchildren and our children.

I love you, honey: hugs and kisses until I hear from you to my wife Ginette from your husband, Thomas.

Thomas's response:

My life is going in the wrong direction, and there are problems in my life. I have never been able to resolve or workout. God, today I want to receive the Lord. I want my marriage to be healed, and I want my business to prosper. Still, before I know, I can have the prosperity of the King.

I have to confess and forsake my sins, and you are here, and you want to go somewhere, and God wants to take you there.

Still, you have to deal with the King's demands, to accept his invitation, and he will make you a king and a queen. Just like that, right now, some of us have a life that is slipping through our fingers like the sands of time.

And despite all you're trying, the more you try, the more it gets away from you. All you have to do is give King Jesus the chance to bring you to the Royal table of riches.

And you can live a life from heaven that will grant you overwhelming blessings. You are as wealthy because of my Father's house, and the architect of the ages designs many mansions. Who only has entered into the minds of men: all you have to do is accept the

King's blessings for a new life. I love you, my precious Guardian Angel treasure from the North Country.

Thomas's response:

Sweetheart, retirement is not in my character: if it were, I would be a man without worth: you are my life. I am in love with you, and showing my love for you is retirement. I am a dead man.

You are my girl, and I'm in love with you. I always have been as

God has shown us, I love you. And I feel showing my love for you in taking the time to offer you my love is a life worth living.

If this were the perfect world, there would be no reason to have a God. The stronger the storm we come through, the more we are going to be blessed by God.

My priority in life is my love for you that will never change: if I take a timeout to retire from our love for each other, that is when it will get boring and not worth living. I choose not to withdraw from our passion because it is precious a gift from God, and the beloved children we are going to have are a gift from God. Your mother is a gift from God.

I understand you are busy, and I am working differently, then we can come together in our passion and remain healthy and build on that love through Jesus Christ, our Lord, and Savior.

The sacrifice I make for you and our love for each other is well worth the effort, and for you making me a better man that God would have me to be for you and your mother. But a labor of love that we will always cherish and thank God for that.

Please do not feel angry with yourself or frustrated because Satan would like you to do it. And where he would like you to go, and we have been there before, we have both danced with the devil. We choose not to look back at those times, only to become stronger warriors for God, in our Christianity, and our love for one another.

We are not into our pride or ego, and we do not care what others think about us except the ones we love, your mother, and our love.

Because if we stop to please others, we are not pleasing God. Others do not judge our thoughts, our words, or actions. What we fail to do: only God will do that, through Jesus Christ, our Lord's name, and the Holy Spirit.

We are two active Christians in love with each other through the miracles of God. We have come together to help many other souls get to where we are going to heaven together. And our children will be a testimony through the Grace of God.

Beauty is a gift freely given by God, such as our love for one another and not for anyone else. We have not been brought together to impress or to let other people, places, or things rent space in — our heads.

There is only room for one another, your mother and, that we will be a witness to many others through the miracle and the testimony.

We do not have to act a certain way: all we have to do to show our love for one another, which we are building on and making more critical day by day. You are the only one in my life right now that I love and care about because I have witnessed the miracle of God working through you. And through your persistence and tenacity, I have held onto this love through thick and thin.

And for that, I cannot thank you enough: you are the love of my life, the love I have never known, and we have never experienced in our lives. And we give thanks to God and Jesus Christ, our Lord's name, who died on the cross for our sins.

John 3: 16. For God so loved the world that he gave his only begotten Son that whoever should believe in Him should not perish but have everlasting life. This verse tells us that there is a hell, and there is a heaven.

And it shows our Faith together in God through Jesus Christ, his only Son, our Lord, we are going to heaven along with your mother. Both of our fathers, your Father, and my Father, have brought us together through the Holy Spirit and Eternal Grace of God, and they are our guardian angels.

And you are going to be a testimony to this whole family with the birthdate, a miracle that my Father will be a testimony to this family. That you were meant to be in our life together with one another, we have our fathers' blessings through the Holy Spirit and Jesus Christ, our Lord, and Savior.

The word retirement is not even in our lives and never will. United together, we have an experience that will be exceptionally blessed and busy doing our Father's work on this earth, the short time we are here together.

I pray continuously, and I have sacrificed for our love. I cannot thank you enough, sweetheart, for making me a better man. Then I could ever have dreamed of, and only because of you, and our love for one another, your persistence in hanging on to our passion.

Why this beautiful lovely lady hangs onto our love by what seems to be a thread, because of the things I have said in the past, for the life of me.

This shows me how much love you have for me, and listening to you on the telephone that one morning at work — asking me, "if I still loved you"? And I could hear the sobbing, hurt, and pain in your voice when you said that.

Yet you dared to ask me and call me on the telephone while you were working on asking that question.

Said to me, this woman loves unconditionally and that I better take this love seriously, or God will not answer any of my prayers.

You are my girl, you are my Angel, I am in love with you, and I love you, and your mother I care very much for she is a woman of excellent knowledge and wisdom. And has a lot of power through prayer with God, our Father. Hugs and kisses

Thomas's response:

And I'm not sure what I am going to name the book, "excruciating soul pain" possibly, introduction: Ginette wanted to remind Thomas of the times that left an indelible mark upon her mind and hurt her feelings on many occasions that Ginette seems to have not forgotten, unfortunately for Thomas. Ginette informed Thomas that she wanted to give him an examination, so Thomas very sensually slipped down his drawers: Ginette then stood back and, with everything she had, said, "do you remember what you said when you hurt my feelings?"

Thomas said, "no, I do not: please shake my memory." Ginette then said, "here is a small reminder" with the swift hard fast kick, she kicked Thomas right in the testicles as hard as she could: Thomas immediately went down on the ground doubled over in excruciating pain: the pain was so horrific that he had to lie, and said, "I did not say that" barely being able to breathe.

Ginette then said, "get up now before I get out the baseball bat and break your ribs." Thomas getting on his knees and ever so slowly getting up, Ginette did not waste any time as she kicked Thomas again, even harder, this time right in the testicles.

Thomas could not say a word. He was turning blue and gasping for air as he had never felt so much pain in all his life. Ginette said, "stand up and turn around. I'm not finished with you yet." Taking Thomas a couple of minutes to regain consciousness and slowly pulling himself to his feet.

Ginette then said, "turn around and bend over, you worthless man" Thomas was thinking she was going to give him a break and a spanking with a belt. That would have felt ten times better.

In agreement, Thomas said yes, okay sweetheart, Ginette said, "don't sweetheart me, all the times and the things you said to me, it is time for you to pay for your sins." As she proceeded to kick Thomas right between the legs, three to four real hard fast knee snap kicks. As a result, Thomas passed out and never regained consciousness for about two hours.

Barely squinting through his eyes, he could see Ginette waiting again with anticipation of joy and temporary satisfaction. Thomas felt like a part-time Christian praying to God in the time of need and finding out it was a futile effort on his part.

You will have to purchase this book to find out the trials and tribulations agony that Thomas may or may not experience from his beautiful bride Ginette. How much longer will Thomas have to pay for his sins? Well, what do you think? I'll bet you anything Thomas has put a smile on Ginette's face, and Thomas is not sure if he is laughing as hard as Ginette?

Still, Thomas is laughing pretty hard and has more fun with himself. Well, Thomas is not exactly sure if he would call this fun. If Thomas has made Ginette's day and put a smile on her face, it was well worth the effort.

Reluctantly, you may want to share this one with your girlfriends, sweetheart. I'm sure they would enjoy this, believe it or not, Ginette still loves Thomas, and Thomas still loves Ginette to pieces. And Thomas is going to pinch Ginette's cheeks, see what Ginette makes Thomas think of? I love you, Ginette, because you are my girl.

Thomas is unsure if tonight's mother Diane would appreciate this, smile, only you would know that you precious little beautiful, scrumptious funny fiancé.

Ginette wrote:

Was I like, wow! 6 emails from him? Sorry for my delay as I could not write back right away. I needed to take my time to read word to word so that the time you took to write to me would not just be a swift reply from me.

Thanks for your compliments that I'm beautiful, actually people say I am, but I do not consider beauty from outside. Still, I mostly look within: the inner beauty is the real beauty. A good character of a person makes them complete the beauty process and makes them a whole. So thanks for seeing with your physical and spiritual eyes that I am beautiful.

I agree I was born too late, and I wouldn't blame my mom! Lol, and I think your mom was in a hurry, or you were in a hurry to come before me. The good part is that we both were still able to meet, aren't we? Good, you realize that it is not too late for us even though there's an age difference: what matters is for us to love each other from the depth of our hearts.

And I promise you I want to love you from the deepest part of my heart to give you the love you have not had from women you have met. I also want you to shower me with love that I have never had from my ex. I wouldn't hesitate to marry you: I have already accepted you in my heart and would marry you, and God willing, I can have children for you.

Thomas, you prove how much you love me without a doubt, and I can feel it! Waking up at 3 a.m. to write makes me think so much about you, regarding the same way I do for you. I do not know why such a strong feeling for you: I wanted to tell my friends about you. Still, I decided not to do that, and most girls would like to discourage me from loving you. They might think I am kidding, but they do not know what goes on in my heart: we all are young. Still, we all do not have the same desires, so better, and I keep what is important to myself until I am ready to leave here to come to you.

I, too, want to get married to you as soon as possible, and I think that is something I have to start thinking about to come to you. I want to be able to meet you before the course of this year, we will see. I need to settle a few things before I can come over to you.

I have heard of the kinder weather there, compared to Canada, so that I would love it there. I hope you are not near where there is a crime. We here in Canada have lived in a peaceful country. We hear so about so much corruption there in the U.S.

Oh yeah, I had fun with my girlfriends last weekend, and the girl in the first pic with me is called Nicole and the second girl is a friend of Nicole her name is Sandra, they are amazing friends, but there are things I do not tell them. Well, I try to be happy as much as I can: thinking so much would have you depressed that's why I do try to put a smile on my face each day.

I realized now why you started behaving strangely a few days ago, and I do not blame you at all. You see, people do not wait to meet you or come closer to someone to know what kind of person he or she is. But when they see your physical appearance, they will go forward to put you in a shadow world, or like my mom would say, paint you black.

From what you say about that lady, I feel sorry that she does not understand when both people saved through the gospel of Jesus Christ: such people would have the same heart.

Ginette wrote:

Hello Darling Thomas,

I am always looking forward to hearing from you, and it brings so much smile to me that you think so much about me. I do as well, and whenever I hear from you and know that you are doing good, it makes me happy. How's your day going? I hope all is going great. I'm sorry, and it broke my heart when I read that you were going to two funerals. Was it your friends or relatives that passed?

I would be the happiest person to be married, and it would make my girlfriends want to get married as well: I want to be an example for the rest to follow.

So yes, I look up to marrying you, my love. I also think about how it would be when we start living together. I have a mixed feeling, happiness, and being nervous as I have never been without my mom and marrying someone. It would be my very first experience, and I look up to that.

All your names have significant meanings. I don't even know the importance of only Ginette since it's originally Anna from the Bible and the story.

I will try to make my way on yahoo. I'll let you know, my love. You amaze me so much with all the romantic words, and I tell you the truth. I was so excited, and I still feel it. I must hold my heart till I reach because I'm not going to fall for any other man apart from you. You're a romantic guy, and you make me fall deeper for you. Have a beautiful day, my love, and know that I'm here thinking about you. I have to go back to work.

Thomas wrote:

Ginette,

While I was researching the distance from where you live to where we will be living.

I love your middle name, and please do not be nervous. I would like you to feel confident and safe with compassion and love to meet a soul mate. Through the grace of God has put us together. Worried or fear is the opposite of faith, and I know in my heart you have the confidence you can feel safe.

God is watching over you: you're such a precious child and so innocent that God would never let anything happen to you. I will treat them with great respect and kindness with compassion and love trusting his love. I am so anxious to be with you.

I love you so much and would like to marry you: that would be God's will for the two of us. I feel that in my heart and spiritually, we are connected. We are yoked spiritually together forever, not until death do us apart until reunited in heaven. We will grow and love and love each other in the way that God would want.

I wish you were here right now, and we were married so I could love you and take care of you. I understand your feelings about meeting someone for the first time and your uneasiness about doing so. Pray to God and no in your heart that you will be protected, cherished with compassion, love, and trust. I love you so much, Ginette: God bless with respect, have a good day. I will get back to you. I love my wife. God bless Thomas.

Ginette wrote:

Hey Thomas,

Sorry if it has taken me a while to write back. You know my schedule makes it a bit difficult to respond right away, and I hope you don't mind. Yes, Ginette or Anna is the same, and it's no problem at all calling me Ginette. The story behind the name makes me also love it, and I feel so good having you call me that.

You are always on my mind, and there's nothing you do that would make me push you away: you're a nice person, and that is what counts. Forget about your physical appearance or age, and I mainly look at your qualities of a truly handsome man and one with a heart for others. A heart full of gold, you may not know that you are unique in your way.

I appreciate the fact that you are a knowledgeable and respectful person to me. I want to make you feel like a king Thomas, you are the right person, and my heart tells me always. I always pray about us, and as I do, my heart feels pleased. I sometimes consider a few other things, but then when I think positively about you and me. I feel more relief than when I want to find items negatively.

I got your version of the story of Job, and I don't think it's going to happen to either of us. Yes, I know in our judgment about each other we have to judge with the love that Christ instructed. Not from our feelings, and they say the right things do not come so quickly. And that is what we are trying so hard to make it come to the past so that we can have a great testimony. Without any struggle, it is impossible to have a piece of compelling evidence.

You're right, and I'm someone that appears at first to people like I am not a determined person. Some not serious when you see my physical appearance. I live my life not to please a man.

Still, my God who sees in secret, I am not a hypocrite that lives in the eyes of men. With all this, you always respect me and show me love: that's one reason I am also open to you and loving you each day. You may wonder why such a beautiful young lady falls for you? It is because you are a great person that understands life on a wide range. And for me, I do not look at things as everyone sees them, but careful observation and simple people make me like them much.

So never think you're not necessary, you are, and I like you to know that before I developed wishing for you, I did consider a few things.

You're so amazing, and I read carefully each verse of the Bible you mentioned: they are all so real. Not every young girl thinks the same way: I think mostly about someone that cares and loves me, and one I will feel the same.

Wow sounds nice reading about your town. I want to live in such a place, as long we can visit the big cities sometimes it would be fine as well. Well, you would be well received here: I have told my Mom whenever I go, she's happy that you're a mature and, after all, a good Christian.

Well, since you're mostly on Yahoo messenger, my lunch break would be the best time. So whenever I go for lunch, I will try from time to time to check on there for you. Yes, I know without faith, there are no possibilities to have what you especially for a Christian. So I always apply belief: I forget what I think I know: the important thing is to allow God to take the lead: that's how I live my life.

That would be nice if we can have children, and I think those guys you talked to were friendly, and from what I read, I think there will be a possibility. I would be glad to talk to them. I love you so much, Thomas, and I like you assured me that we have a long life together.

Well, it wouldn't be an issue to stay at home and look after. I don't think it would be fair to live in instead of living with you under the same roof. I may also work because I am a reliable person who doesn't believe in looking only at my husband. Thanks for your number, and since I have it now, I'll give you a call whenever I want to get in touch.

This way, it would be easier to get in touch faster if we do not have the chance to keep in touch by email: sometimes, both methods aren't an issue. I will also keep you in my prayers for God to give you wisdom so that you can shine your light on others. I know thousands, not millions of people looking to your publications around the world or the country.

We put everything in God's hands, and the rest will follow. I know by the help of God all we will come to the past.

It was so lovely hearing from you, Thomas, and you have a blessed day. Enjoy the rest of your day: hugs and kisses from your favorite girl Ginette.

Thomas wrote:

I just wrote you a long email and lost it, so here we go again, sweeter than honey. You're asking about the funerals. I have one tomorrow. A friend of mine just passed on last Wednesday, and he was a great musician and a phenomenal carpenter, and a hard worker.

And a lady friend I went to high school with passed on about a week ago she was married to a good friend. Do not feel sorry I call in the celebration of life. We will be together again, but not yet.

You and I have a life to live in love to give one another through the grace of God and Jesus Christ, the Lord's name. I love you so much, Ginette, and I miss you so much. I will try to have a plan, picking you up from the airport that we get married on the way to our home.

Please do not feel uncomfortable or nervous: that is the opposite of faith. I would want you to feel safe, secure with compassion, and love with me. I love you, Ginette, and I would like for you to be my wife. I cannot say how much I love you and have compassionate care for you. You are a precious angel, God that I prayed for years I have been praying for you. When I prayed to God, I got the message that this is my soulmate. God loves us that much. I have spiritual feelings and love for you: we are equal in the presence of God.

I will take care of you provide for you with compassion and respect. I will love you as you have never loved before, and you will love to be loved the way I will love you. God bless with love and prayers. I love you, Ginette, and I always will. We're going to have a great life together while I was checking the distance between our locations from your area to our site.

Ginette wrote:

Hi, Thomas my Love,

We kept missing each other on Yahoo messenger, and I feel sad about that. It isn't your fault, really, but me, it's me having to go to work and drive back home. At that time, you may have already left online. Instead of giving a call, I sometimes forget that it would have been easier if your phone were texting. I would text to let you know to connect online, but it's not so bad because we still hear from each other, even my busy time.

How are you doing today? I hope you're having a beautiful day. Mine is working, but it is going great. I wrote to you on Yahoo messenger telling you the time difference. So once you know the time difference and the time I am home, I don't think we will have to miss each other. I am home from 6:30 p.m.—Canadian time.

I look to connecting with you soon. Have a blessed day, and know you're the only person in my heart right now. And you make me so happy with your sweet messages, you're such a lovely guy, and you have stolen my heart completely. I can't believe you did, but that's true, and I love you so much. I look to chatting soon, my sweet man — warm hugs and kisses from me, Your love Ginette.

Thomas wrote:

I pray you are doing well this morning. Can I ask you a question, please? And I would certainly understand, I have been living alone for 4 years, and I devote my life to God and service, and I will not ever talk to you in a way that I did yesterday. As I mentioned before, when I buy a pair of shoes, I do not try them on. I believe them first, take them home and have the faith that they will fit. The communication between the conversation and the companionship through chatting with you was well worth the effort. I love you for that, and I have great compassion for you: I care.

I have written about the grace of love of biblical proportion that only you and I can have together forever and eternally with the grace of God.

Do not forget to show hospitality to strangers, for by doing so, some have shown hospitality to angels without knowing it. And I thank you for the reception that you have shown me. I feel you are an angel, and I did not know it. Forgiveness and repentance in the Bible is the reason Jesus Christ came and taken all our sins. How many times must you forgive your neighbor who sins against you? Jesus said's 7×49

I love you because you're worth it, and God loves you, and I will see you one day in heaven. We will be together for the simple reason I have never communicated with a lady, such as yourself. It was like Christmas morning, and a dream come true for me. You have a good day, and I know you're busy to take your time, and I am more than likely wrong with my assumption, as most of us are. Ginette, with the grace of God and our prayers through the Holy Spirit and Jesus Christ, our Lord's name. I find myself drawing closer to you than a soul mate God would have for one another.

I will write more on messenger as opposed to emails like we have both mentioned before: we may, at one point, be able to talk or chat with each other on Yahoo messenger. I love you, I care about you, and I think about you more often than not.

And one day soon, God willing, we will be together, and I thank God for that. Inspiring our lives together is a God-given gift that we should be very thankful for: God bless with love and prayers, your husband, Thomas. I am going to resend this, not sure if you received this precious email. I believe you did: I would talk more messenger, my angel. God bless with love and prayers: your friend always Thomas.

Ginette wrote:

Hi Thomas,

I'm sorry you did lose your precious message you wanted to send. It's not still wrong, and I'm the one to apologize for my delay. Things have been a little busy for me, but thank God I can message you now. How's it going with you? I hope you have been doing great, always thinking about you and missed you much, and it feels so good to hear from you each time. With the help of God, I'm excellent and not much to complain about.

Reading your message, I see many funerals, but as you say, not to feel sorry. Yes, I agree with no matter who we have lost in this world, shortly in eternity, we will surely be together. It's sure a celebration of life after death. Well, you and I are thinking the same way: we are not going to die now: there's still a great future ahead for you and me. And I look forward to being your wife and spending our lives together.

Well, I'm not nervous or will ever be: I know you're a great person and what I understand about you each day tells me you're a very caring and romantic person. I would never be nervous, hoping they tell you positive news. Have you heard any news from them yet?

Oh, the airfare must be so cheap: I'll find out about it as well. I just finalized a few things as well about applying for a passport and other documentation. Prices change daily, so hopefully, when the time is right, we will be lucky. Do you love my middle name? Thanks for liking it: but I haven't picked it for a long time, but I appreciate it since you do now.

Yes, I too can not wait to be in your arms, I can feel a strong desire you have for me from afar, and I pray that all we have asked for will come to pass.

Thanks so much for all the kind words, my love, and you have a great day. I wrote to you on yahoo messenger and hoped we could also catch each other on there. Hearing from one another from both ways makes me happy. I love you so much.

Hugs and kisses from me. You have a great time until I hear from you — your Ginette.

APRIL 2018, ROMANTIC MEMOIRS FROM HEAVEN

April 16, 2018

Ginette wrote:

Hello to the best man in my world!

I hope you're having a great Sunday! Mine went great, and I could relax a bit since I didn't work today and yesterday. I was in a hurry yesterday when I wrote to you as I wasn't sure my message would come through since my service provider was facing some technical problems.

You're right: we understand each other, and I'm always going to be the one that understands you even if the rest of the people do not seem to follow you. It's because their spirits and yours are not compatible. In this world, not everyone was made actually to understand another person unless God leads you to.

The heartfelt words you put in there speak volumes about you and the character you have. You're such a lovely person, and I'm convinced that you're truly the love of my life!

Thinking about you, you and you enjoy the rest of your day. With regards. Hugs and kisses from your one and only Me.♥

Thomas wrote:

Just a love story between the two of us, and we love each other so much, and it is a God-given gift. And we are patiently waiting for the time when we will get together and make love with each other.

We are sick in love, and then we go and do it again, all night long, we love each other so.

How much, you like that, don't you? I can love you with compassion, compared to a love you have never had before, and I have never experienced before. I cannot wait for you to be my wife. So we can love each other and take care of one another. I will be so perfect with the spirit of God, and everything will be okay because it is love.

I cannot get enough of how you would like to be loved and how you would like me to love you. Tell me how you would like me to love you? I think about you continuously, of love, and compassion we will have for one another. Through God, Jesus Christ, and the Holy Spirit working through us. Growing in love and becoming more and more in love every day with one another and helping others.

Set an example of what a. loving husband and wife through the spirit will set the standard for others. Ginette, I love you so much sweetheart, I can hardly wait for us to be together. You are my wife for the rest of our lives, and into eternity we will be together. I love the way you love me, so beautifully, and you're so sweet. I cannot get enough of you in the way you love me.

I pray you're doing well, and God bless you with love and prayers, your husband, Thomas. I sent you a long Yahoo messenger, and I pray you to read. I would like to talk to you on the telephone at some point in time at your convenience. I can either call you, or you can call me. Or we can video chat, and I miss you.

I think about you all the time. If you read my Yahoo video chat, I had written a long chat message that you may be interested in. I pray that you are and that I have not offended you in any way.

I first looked up your middle name, and as you had mentioned at one point in time, you did not like it. And then I did some research and thanked God I did. The research I did of your middle name had taken on a whole new meaning.

I know you're busy, and I understand that. So do not ever be sorry for not getting back to me right away, okay. You are a sweetheart, and you're my soul mate in the love of my life. I pray that you feel the same way about me.

I'm looking forward to taking care of you with compassion and love and helping others by setting an example of our relationship that we will have together.

And if you read the Yahoo messenger, God willing, if it does not happen, the mission we have in life together will be well worth the effort.

If you look up the content of your middle name, by the way, I love it: it gives us both a purpose. God's grace through Jesus Christ, our Lord, the Holy Spirit, is working through both of us to help others.

I love you, sweetheart, you are my soul mate, now, forever, and eternity we will be in heaven. Together on God's green earth with love and compassion for one another that is God's will for us. I pray you to feel the same way. God bless you, honey, with God's love and prayers, Thomas. Do not forget to say your prayers.

Ginette wrote:

Hello Darling Thomas,

I am always looking forward to hearing from you, and it brings so much smile to me that you think so much about me. I do as well, and whenever I hear from you and know that you are doing good, it makes me happy. How's your day.

Thomas wrote:

Ginette, I know you're busy. I have to wait for my wife anxiously. Do not feel sorry for not getting back to me: you're my favorite girl and only girl.

Can you please excuse me if I have said anything to have offended you? Like some men tell you, anything you want to hear just to get into your pants. Those were not my intentions, and we are equally yoked with God and Jesus Christ, our Lord, with the Holy Spirit working through us.

And my love for you, this is why we are equally yoked spiritually. I genuinely believe that God meant for us to be together for that reason. Together we can save souls, and I feel this in my heart. And the way we communicated with each other, God has let us both know. I love you and care about you with compassion from my heart and the spirit. God bless you with love and prayers, Thomas.

I just sent you an email: you might check your emails and read them. You have a good day, in my prayers are with you. God bless, with love and blessings: your friend always Thomas.

Can we still be friends? We are both Christians, and forgiveness is the key to love. Do not forget to show hospitality to strangers, for by so doing, "some people have shown hospitality to angels without knowing it." Offering hospitality to an angel whom I do not know and have not met: by the grace of God, I thank you.

Yahoo Messenger: Romantic Conversation Between Thomas And Ginette.

Ginette wrote:

Hi my love

Thomas wrote:

Hi, sweetheart, thank you very much for calling. I appreciate that you are a great lady, and my humblest apology for my stinking thinking.

Ginette wrote:

You're welcome, my love.

Thomas wrote:

Can you please forgive me? I had you mixed up with another lady.

And she talked just like you did, very similar but not accurately, no one can speak like a — Christian, like you and I can, when I mention your name to her, Ginette, the conversation stopped suddenly. There are more scammers on this computer.

Ginette wrote:

Give me 5 minutes

Thomas wrote:

Do not let me frustrate you for typing so fast, okay? Take your time, and You sounded so sweet on the phone. I could have jumped right through the phone and pulled you right through the phone lines. Married, we have two children together, and live a life with you, growing in love with God's grace: I pray I do not frustrate you with my program Dragon? As fast as I talk it types, it breaks my heart to hurt your feelings.

April 17, 2018

Ginette wrote:

I'm back.

Thomas wrote:

How are you, sweetheart? Did you read all of my messages?

Ginette wrote:

You don't frustrate me at all, just that when you write too many words. I get a bit confused lol, pulse what you said today about someone that pretended to be me.

April 18, 2018

Ginette wrote:

Hi, my love: I tried calling, but it seems like you're not home, so try to sign on yahoo when you get back.

Thomas wrote:

Hi, my beautiful wife, how are you? I was home. You just have to leave a message. I do not pick up the phone because of the advertisement if you leave a message and say that this is Ginette. I will pick you up if I'm not home. I will let you know, okay? Let us pray to God that it will work: God's will, we can have a couple of children. I would love nothing better than to have children with you and raise the family.

I have been working on another book about Christianity. Did you check your emails? I am doing a lot of research about the Bible and the end times prophesied to be the year 2018, the year of our Lord. And you can see that the world situation is not getting better.

Did I ask you properly? "Ginette, will you marry me?"

It is 5:10 pm here now: if you want me to talk to you sooner,

I will or anytime at your convenience, sweetheart. I love you and think about you a lot, and I am informing other people about you and me getting married. I pray you do not mind: the few people

I have talked to about it thought it would be a good idea for both of us since we are Christians. They want to help other people save souls, start a ministry together, and have children together.

I am the sperm donor, God willing, smile, unite together, and have some children from God. That will help us, and they will know more than we will, as children always do.

Ginette wrote:

Why is it arrogant?

Thomas wrote:

1/10 people are selfish, taking Greek mythology and college: most of our psychology comes from Greek mythology. Narcis rejected Mima's love, and for doing so, God, Zeus made narcissists looked in a pool of water for eternity: it is called the reflective love of self.

Similar to Satan, who thought he was better than God. Anyway, the statistics are 1/10 people are selfish. There is no cure: they only think of themselves, and they make other people's lives miserable, in a weird psychological way.

Those people cannot be helped, and they are precisely like Satan, who thought he was better than God. God made Satan the most beautiful angel, and Satan thought he could take over heaven.

You must know some narcissistic people, or have met them real arrogant, think they know everything. And believe that you are an ignorant person, those people we just have to pray for, and not be around them. They are evil and will make you feel guilty or bad about yourself.

I'm not that familiar with iPhones since I have two desktop computers, iMac G5's:

It is tranquil where we will live in our home together: you're going to love it here: it is so beautiful.

Ginette wrote:

You're right: there are such people, and I have had friends like that, very jealous of others and arrogant.

I'll find out if I can get the dragon app. I'll let you know I love calm communities.

Thomas wrote:

Please, it would be far easier for us to communicate: it has to be quiet to use Dragon. The phone cannot ring: people cannot be around talking.

I do not hear a car go by, and I do not understand a horn: it is complete silence, I call it God's country. When you get here, you will have to agree. If you get onto what is a global map, you will see the country for yourself. I mentioned to you that there could be 5000 people, instead of 500 living in this area. Everyone knows me, or my family, or our family. I have to get used to saying us, and our, and my wife, spent years waiting for you.

Ginette wrote:

Yes, you told me about the town with 500 people. 500 or 5000?

Thomas wrote:

5000 it used to be 500

Ginette wrote:

I'm glad we have each other. The population has increased then.

Thomas wrote:

I am so happy, and it is like Christmas morning: you're a Miracle, the grace of God, and an answer to my Prayer. It is a resort town, where the people who have summer homes. A well-known last name, with consideration, kindness, and compassion. That name others will treat you with respect: everyone in our family helped people for nothing. And watched our family grew up hard, having to work for everything to keep food on the table. To keep it, we must give it back, and we came into this world with absolutely nothing. We will be leaving the same way, except for the legacy of our children, God willing.

Ginette wrote:

I can imagine, and yes, you make me feel special, and I would be so happy with you. I don't want to be a stranger in your town.

Thomas wrote:

You are far beyond my imagination and most certainly a miracle through the grace of God coming into my life, as I have been praying for a soul mate. An honest soul mate who loves God, you are my miracle. I am so excited thinking about you all the time: it is almost unbelievable, but my faith is Unshakable.

I know nothing is impossible with God, and yes, we will be so happy together: we will set an excellent example for others. And, in doing so, just by observing the way we treat each other. And we are planting the seed of God and the Holy Spirit that dwells within.

The love we have for one another will make others want what we have. The knowledgeable lady, I am proud of you because you're worth it. I love you because God loves you and God both of us: we are God's miracles.

If you get tired, sweetheart, do not hesitate to get some rest: it must be about 8:45 pm there. I have been going through my computer. I'm sure you understand how much stuff we can keep on the network of old email addresses and con artists ladies' contacts. I never realized there was so much on my computer. Here comes somebody.

Ginette wrote:

No worries, lol I'll do it at nine: chatting with you is beautiful, and I feel close to you each time!

Thomas wrote:

Know it is a friend of mine named Frank.

Ginette wrote:

Hmm really?

Thomas wrote:

Yes, Frank owns the limousine service, and when you get here, he can give us a tour in his limousine. He would be more than happy to Frank knows all the cool sites: he just agreed with me.

Ginette wrote:

Sounds nice: I will be treated like a presidential candidate, lol.

Thomas wrote:

You're precisely right, and Frank said he would be more than happy to take us around. Knows were all the great lookouts sites, and the best ones, tourists he takes all over. So he knows where all the best locations are, restaurant sightseeing.

Frank has three limousines, and he loves to drive, so you will most certainly be treated like presidential royalty. I had to tell Frank to be quiet because everything he said was typed. So he went out in the guesthouse, where I have a veteran friend of mine staying in a wheelchair, and Frank brought him some groceries.

So it is just you and I now sweetheart, I love you so much, and it is about time for you to get some rest, think you have three minutes, or we do: I love you so much. We will have our privacy when others know that we are married and living together: it will be you and I unless we invite other people over.

Ginette wrote:

Wow, you have an excellent plan for me, and I'm so glad to ever meeting you, my love. I'll go to get a shower and head to bed.

Ginette wrote:

Nite Okay.

Thomas wrote:

A big kiss and a big hug and in bed with you putting my arms around you and talking to you and loving you and loving you. Beware, we may wear each other out, smile consensually with God's grace, and love my precious angel a miracle child of God's.

An answer to my Prayer, I love you so much I will more than likely keep on chatting, and I will talk to you tomorrow about 5 pm my time unless you would like me to speak to you earlier.

I could call you on the telephone, I do have your telephone number, or would you feel more comfortable just chatting for a while? You know writing and chatting to one another reaches into the — creases of our mind.

Ginette wrote:

I'll let you know when, as long I'm home, Good night.

Thomas wrote:

Remember when you call me, and the answering machine picks up. Just say this is Ginette, and I will pick the phone right up, good night, honey.

Ginette wrote:

Okay, I'll.

Thomas wrote:

Now I lay me down to sleep I pray the. Lord, my soul, to keep, and if I should die before I wake. I pray the Lord, my soul, to take. God grant me the serenity to accept the things I cannot change, the courage to change the things I can, and the wisdom to know the difference.

And protect Ginette, she is your precious child God, an answer to my Prayer. I know You will, and for that, I thank You through Jesus Christ, name amen. Can I eat your picture? Smile. Should I say kiss your picture and kiss your image very tenderly?

April 19, 2018

Thomas wrote:

Ginette, I pray you are doing well, I will look forward to chatting with you. It will be 5 pm my time, and 8 pm your time. You do realize that you are a miracle, the precious answer to my Prayer? And I pray to God that I can take care of you, make you the happiest lady that God would want. I love God through Jesus Christ, our Lord's name, and praying to the Holy Spirit that answers our prayers.

I could never have expected that God would put a lady like you into my life, and in God's eyes through grace, means a gift freely given of God. I believe, and I have the faith that God will make this the happiest spiritual of love, and Prayer, that He could ever have for two people. I love you, Ginette. Ginette, check the emails that I sent for you today through the Holy Spirit inspired me to love you.

Ginette, my humblest apologies: can you please forgive me? I went to lay down at 3:30 pm, and I just woke. Sleeping, I love you. I will tell you that every day, we should never go one day without saying, we love one another. It just makes the day seem a little better and shows the one you love.

You never know if and when we will ever get to communicate again. God will come like a thief in the night we know not when. I'm going to wait here a few more minutes, and I should wait longer than that, about 15 or 20 minutes. I do not know why this friend of mine staying in the guesthouse, Frank. I believe I mentioned him to you a veteran, also take him to an Alcoholics Anonymous meeting tonight, and we missed that, just to get the both of us out of here.

I think we will go to town and pick a couple of hamburgers.

I'm not sure if he is awake or even wants to go, I will be back in a minute my precious sweet angel. If ladies that I have talked to about you, and they feel I am the luckiest man alive. I say no such thing as luck: this was intuitively meant to be by God.

And that on some level that nothing happens for nothing, we both prayed about this. I'll be back in about 10 minutes, and I'm going on the front porch and yelling at Frank to see if he still wants to go. Back in a minute, anyway, it's Friday night you may be out with girlfriends, and whatever you do, have fun.

I'm very sporadic, and I have been that way for the last 4 years.

Looking forward to getting married to my soul mate, and we will have a tight schedule, I'm sure. Possibly we will just have to turn it over to God and see what he has in mind for us. God bless with love and prayers, your husband.

I always enjoyed writing to the one I love, and just a little irritated with myself. That I fell sound asleep and was not able to speak or chat with my precious Ginette.

How did your day go? I pray that it went well, and everything is okay in your life: I love you: you're worth it, God loves you.

One more thing, sweetheart, I will be up for a while so that the spirit moves you, and you feel like calling me. Let me know if you would like to chat. I should be available although, God willing, I will be I have your telephone number, I could call you. I do not want to do that if it's not a convenient time for you. So whenever it's a convenient time for you, please feel free to try, thank you.

I'm a little frustrated, however: I will turn it over to God and pray about it: let us pray together, okay. I love you.

It breaks my heart and hurts my soul to even think or mention this to you. That we have already made and commitment to ourselves and God, we should follow through with, I feel. I just feel obligated to mention it to you, that if you ever change your mind. It seems like It is going to be too hard to move to Arizona, and be with me, your God's precious angel. We can always be friends, no matter what. So if sometimes in your life, and we never know what is going to come up in our life. You could meet a nice young gentleman.

I care you're worth it, your precious angel of God, and if I did anything to hurt you or harm you or hurt your feelings. Or you did not feel comfortable with anything, and God would make sure that I paid for that, in one way or another. God would say, why did you not take care of one of my special Angels that you prayed for, I sent to you? What would I say to God? You do not say anything to God, except pray and be fearful of his wrath and power.

I believe that if God ever asked me that question, I would be damned to hell. God does not ask questions, he gives the answers: we pray, as in Jesus Christ, our Lord's name. Think about the suggestion, one thing I would never want is for you to be unhappy, in any way, in any situation. I would treat you with compassion, love with respect for our God.

April 20, 2018

Ginette wrote:

Hi, Thomas, not sure you're here sorry about last night I was tired, and I think I'm a bit late. I have read all your messages and will wait a bit to see if we can chat, if not, then it's tomorrow.

April 21, 2018

Thomas wrote:

> *Ginette, my humble his apology, you and I must be spiritually connected along the same waves. I was tired of myself, and I apologize for not getting back to you sooner. Once again, can you please forgive me? Another suggestion and how you feel about it, and I'm not making any excuses. You are as crazy as I am, smile, that we both do not waste life, not doing anything is a waste of life.*
>
> *We are willing to try anything to live this life to our fullest as God would have us do: we only come this way once. Anyway, my suggestion is that you come to Arizona, and stay with me for a week or two or how long you would like. And just get to know one another and see if you're going to love this lifestyle.*
>
> *There may be character defects only because of our age, that would not be compatible or maybe. Just think about it anyway: what I miss most in the last years is not lying next to a lady. Just putting my arm around her and talking to her in bed with her clothes.*
>
> *I have done some research, and when a couple starts to kiss, it will inevitably lead to making love together. Or, we could just get married as planned and start living our life together, and once again, can you please forgive me.*
>
> *I think about you daily, and I want the best for your life, you are so young and beautiful. You have a lot of life left in front of you, as I feel I do as well. To make amends to our God and write together.*
>
> *Frank, the limousine driver friend of mine, who will possibly be a friend of ours. Is looking forward to driving us to all the sites around Arizona. And go to the most beautiful, restaurants, and places.*
>
> *I have been to three funerals in the last 2 to 3 months, and I have one more coming up June 10. I usually make a video of music, pictures, and pass them out to family and friends, and that takes time. I will send you three videos of people that have passed on recently — friends of mine, and one more good friend who just passed on. I just called his wife and ask her if I could have about 20 pictures to put together a CD, which not finished yet.*

You will get used to me, my sick sense of humor that will make you laugh. So hang on to your pants, only kidding, I think, maybe I will. Perhaps I won't, could be that I will, possibly. Anyway, my crazy little wife, I love you, and God bless you with love and Prayer, your husband, Thomas.

What I was trying to say earlier is that if you decide to come out and just visit, I would love to play with you in bed all night. And just talk, put my arms around you, and fall asleep together, can we do it without kissing?

That will lead to making love, therefore: not married in the sight of God, we could be doing an injustice to our souls and their eternal destination. Or God might have us do more work for him, by placing some thorns in the flesh, for breaking his laws. Do you think you could contain yourself under those circumstances?

And I'm not sure that would be one of the most tempting situations, I would ever have been. And I think Satan would be right there egging us on. I would enjoy hearing your thoughts, and when is your birthday again? My beautiful wife.

My great Christian friend Ginette for always and eternity. I have been doing is working on a computer for a friend of mine. Staying out of the guesthouse: he is in a wheelchair.

A gunner on a helicopter who gave us United States Marines a ride to hell whenever we needed one. Or if we were shot up, and injured, they would transport us back to the base camp.

April 22, 2018

Ginette wrote:

Hi, my love. Sorry for my delay, I was got back home from visiting friends, and I just read your sweet messages. I'm so excited to hear from you once again. How are you doing?

Thomas wrote:

Ginette, I'm doing very well thank you for asking, I must give an apology once again, my computer has broken down, and I just got it up and running. How are you doing?

I hope you had fun with your friends. God blessed with love and prayers, love Thomas, my sweet.

I love you so much and think about you continuously. I pray that we can talk tomorrow night, I would try to get on about 5. PM my time. And I would imagine it would be 8 pm your time, have fun and have a good day.

April 23, 2018

Thomas wrote:

Ginette, did you get the two books I sent you? You should have them by now: if not, the wrong address more than likely on them, and sent back. I will resend them again, and I had the lady next door that is married.

Two children, put your address on the outside, and it did not look right, I asked the gentleman at the post office, and he thought it looked okay. Although when she was writing the address, it seemed to be backward, please let me know, thank you I love you.

So do not feel obligated or guilty in any way, please. However, I thank you for the incentive, and God bless you, I love you.

Ginette, are you there, or am I here? Are are you there and I am here? Smile, if you're too tired, I understand, I will talk to you tomorrow. I will be on the computer for a few more minutes, 10 or 15 minutes.

April 24, 2018

Ginette wrote:

Hi, honey, I'm here now Hope you're still there. It is 8:33 here. This is the address I hope the lady got it right, and I'll be here for a while to see if you get back online. I have been wondering why up until now I haven't received your letter.

April 24, 2018

Thomas wrote:

I love you and miss you so much my apology once again, I always say once again.

God loves us, I think about you all the time you know not a day passes when I do not think about being together with you and married and having children together. I get this spiritual feeling that we are going to have two children. I'm going to be around long enough to see our grandchildren.

If anything changes, you happen to go around the corner and run into a young gentleman who is a Christian. He says everything that I would say to you. And treat you with great respect, passion, and care because God loves you. God loves me: I just cannot want to hold you back from an opportunity that you may have one day.

I'm not sure how you feel about that? I'm not trying in any way, shape, or form to disregard our relationship. I want to have children with you. I want to marry you, and want to be together with you. I want you to be happy most of all, and God would want it that way, what am I going to say to God when I get to heaven? Why haven't you take care of one of my God-fearing children, a one-of-a-kind precious angel you prayed? Why did you not take care of her when I answered your Prayer?

I will wait for you, okay I just thought you might have been tired from a long weekend. I was kind of tired myself. I was laying down and fell asleep, and that's no excuse for not talking to my beautiful wife. Thank you for that address again. I am going to send you two more books tomorrow.

I did send with the two books, and some cool bookmarks are the only reason I could think that you would not get the package because they had pennies on them and the metal could have shown up Ginette, I'm going to send you emails every day and the emails we send back and forth between us and the communication if you do not mind.

If you do not remember, I will take out the romantic feelings we had for each other, that is between you and me and God. I'm going to put it together right now and send you what I have and see what you think, okay? We have said some very spiritual godly precious words between the two of us, that others need to talk to each other, the way we communicate and chat. And if it's not okay with you, just let me know, sweetheart.

Sweetheart, my soulmate, I'm here, I'm expecting Frank the limousine driver to bring the other Frank was staying in the guesthouse from the hospital.

Still, it may take a minute, and you come before anyone they will have to wait until you, God, and I finished spiritually connecting. Your way of spiritual discernment, along with ours, will set an excellent example for others.

I'm here sweetheart I miss you so much God bless you you're worth it because God loves you. Your one of his precious angels, only one of you, and we found each other in the dark. I'm getting interrupted continuously. I'm going to lock myself in this bedroom, wishing you were here with me, you're so beautiful.

I keep looking at your pictures.

I love you with the Holy Spirit through Jesus Christ, our Lord's name, and our love that is so precious to show others that miracles can happen. I'm right here, and I will not leave until I hear from you, okay?

So if I do not answer right away, I'm getting an interrupted friend of mine. Frank, coming from the hospital, does not have much longer to live. So I have to have a little compassion, we have to hook up a TV for him he may stay in the hospital again tonight, has been there two days.

What can I do to make you the happiest woman alive with the spiritual discernment coming from God, I'm going to love you and take care of you, treat you like the beautiful precious young lady that you are, you should not expect anything less.

I will wait for you forever, and I'm going back to work. The same address, I just think written down wrong: there may be another problem I sent you a Bunch of Christian bookmarks from the Bible that have metal pennies on them. They may have x-rayed them for one reason or another. I think it's just the wrong address that written down Incorrectly. Start out reading the chapters with the word God in them: those are the miracles. Many more, for instance, you and I meeting through the Holy Spirit is beyond miraculous.

It's something I feel that is a sin against God because God says to subdue the earth and become plentiful as he told Abraham, "his descendants shall be numbered as the stars in the skies." Ginette, you will always be my guardian angel.

I'm sure there is spiritual content that you will either want to add or remove my prayers are with the ones that got ran over by that person in Montréal. That ran over those citizens for no reason. I was sad. I think you must be tired, Ginette. or other things going on in your life it is 5:50 pm here which would make it 8:50 pm there in my right and my right and my right forget it I'm trying to say am I correct

I will be here for a while: do not forget to mention your prayers. God bless with love and prayers to my wife from her husband, Thomas.

If I do not respond, please just call me and say this is Ginette. Like you did before. That made me so happy, and we will meet here on Yahoo messenger. Let me know a convenient time that I can call you, if you would care romance our love on the telephone. If not I understand, I never stop thinking about you. God loves you: you're worth it: you are a special Angel that He created just for myself. And the wife he created just for your husband.

Thomas wrote:

Good night sweetheart good night honey, I will send you an email with the love letter the way we can love each other, only the way we can. You shared a photo, Similar to this. Remember, it's you and me and the love we have for one another that God wants us to have with each other. You are beautiful: why not let your husband see you that way. I'm ready now that we know one another and have plans for our future together, loving one another.

This one is beautiful in it is a God sent a picture, let us say something for our marriage if you agree with that God bless with love and prayers your husband, Thomas. I will let you know when I send the other two books, and I just believe they will be sent back to me, although it takes time to send something back. I'm not waiting. I'm sending you two more Books today with bookmarks that you're going to love Christian bookmarks. I love you.

Ginette, if I'm not available, please give me a call, nothing important I just wanted to know how you felt about the emails that I sent you? With love, God willing, I will be available at 5 pm my time. I love you with compassion and care you shared a photo.

Ginette wrote:

For you, sweetheart.

April 25, 2018

Thomas wrote:

Are you their sweetheart? Ginette, my sweetheart? I am waiting for you where you are? Inquiring minds would love to know, smile God might even like to see where you may be. Did you enjoy the love stories?

I believe you have to be in the mood, so whenever you're in the mood, please do not hesitate to let me know if they were a little risqué. My humblest apologies once again: you realize why I am waiting for you? Because I love you, I will wait, I will wait and I will wait.

I have been waiting for 4 years for my soul mate you are worth it God loves you and your husband does as well.

Scrumptious I can wait I'm not sure if I can wait another 4 years, a little longer than that. I would love to see our grandchildren. This is my fault I was late, I was laying down sleeping, and when I woke up, I said oh darn God help me. You may be reading this story that I sent.

I'm leaving for town, to pick up a few groceries and get some gasoline in my vehicle. I should say our truck. Am I assuming you have a driver's license? And if you do not, we will get you one immediately, if that's okay with you? Maybe you cannot drive, and I will have to drive you everywhere, and that will be just fine.

I would love that the two books are being sent out today, and please let me know when you get them under your alias name. I sent it in your alias name last time, and I'm going to have to get me an alias name, it sounds like fun, smile I love you.

I pray to God, you still love me. We have to set the example for others, although what we do in our bedroom is okay with God, you and I have biblical scripture to prove that.

I would assume that you are tired, and I understand I am leaving in about 10 minutes I will be back in about an hour and 1/2. I know that's too late for you. We will talk to my beautiful precious soulmate wife. I love you by my-passionate-feelings.

Just that I would tell you I love you before I say good night. The books are in the mail, and please let me know when you get them to thank you, sweetheart. You shared three photos just curious do you do any of these ladies

The only reason I'm asking is this relationship is come up with the name Ginette, and one of them is from Toronto, Canada.

Love is trust, and I love you, and I trust you. just curious, that's all whether you knew them or not?

To all of a sudden, switch directions in the middle of the stream, from Anna to Ginette. I'm just a little confused maybe you can explain better to me. I would appreciate that, sweetheart.

Ginette, how are you today, sweetheart? If you're there, I will be here for a while. I do understand talking every day is inconvenient because we have separate lives to live right now. And at times it is difficult.

I look forward to our chats together and loving you the way you would like. I Miss you, and I love you.

Sweetheart, I'm going to lay down for a little while and then go out, to pick up a few groceries. Beautiful, I wish you were here I love you, and we will talk again later God bless with love and prayers Thomas.

Your husband, if you would care to call me, I will be lying down for about 45 minutes, to about an hour before I leave. It is 5:35 pm thank you, sweetheart.

April 16, 2018

Ginette wrote:

Hi honey.

You have written so much, and I like that of how you express yourself each time I wish I could do the same. But I'm not a good writer for you it's what you do every day so I can imagine, you write.

So well and explain in detail, I get so excited about reading your lovely messages. Concerning the girls' pic, you sent me I have no idea at all and thought you asked me the same question the other day. If I knew her and that she was from somewhere, I don't have any idea at all.

Also, I didn't change my name at all, I only gave you what's on my passport, but most people called me Anna, and the name on my yahoo is my Mom's family last name. So I use that just for online hope you understand. I love the name Anna, and I told you, though, I hated the name Ginette. It was my name given by my dad.

Understand that there are thousands, if not millions of Ginette in the world, so don't get confused about that, my love.

I am heading to bed shortly and wouldn't bother you to call: we should chat tomorrow. Know that I love you and praying and hoping that all we wish and pray for will come to pass. Have a good night and sweet dreams.

April 27, 2018

Thomas :

Ginette, I am spiritually attracted to the name Anna: for obvious reasons, it is right out of the Bible. If you would prefer me to call you, I will. And especially to my fiancé, who I am going to marry one day.

I have some good news for us, I got a new doctor yesterday, and I have an appointment with her on May 17.

They always asked me if I would prefer a male or female, Dr.? And I got a sweetheart of a representative talked to me on the telephone yesterday, and I was explaining to her that I did not like the way men treated ladies. And that ladies have. Emotions, feelings, and intuition that men do not have.

For the most part, it's usually the little head that leads the big head around. Smile. She agreed with me on every issue I brought up about men, and she was an older lady I could tell by talking to her On the phone.

Anyway, my doctor, and I explained to you the reason I fired or replaced my mail previous Dr. is that he was narcissistic. I told that also to the representative I talked to yesterday. It's not healthy for a doctor to jump up and down and have A tantrum. And with the lady doctor who I have not met yet, I believe God led her to me.

I have a spiritual feeling that with God working in our life, Dr. will have more compassion for you and I and that we want children together. What do you think?

I realize I had a lot to write, and I have more to write as far as fiction about you, and I. Could call it nonfiction when you and I get together and get married and have children together.

Please keep praying for us, that it be God's will, and that God knows how much we love him. And spiritually, I feel it would be setting an example for the multitudes of people that we will come into contact with. Or that will contact us because of our situation as far as age and having children together.

Only if you feel in the mood and appropriate, I will write more stories about the two of us, and keep in mind we are two of God's precious angels, and there are only two of us. No the other two alike, and we met through the Holy Spirit with God's plan for us for the salvation of others.

Ginette, you do not have to be a good writer: just being with me is going to inspire my writing beyond human comprehension. You're going to bring so much peace and joy into my life. Whether you think you can write or not, you are a phenomenal writer. We will inspire each other, and God will take care of us with compassion and love, and I genuinely have faith.

I could write to you all day, and all night long, you do realize that, of course, my sweet precious angel. And I believe I informed you early that just being a man, I will hurt your feelings unconsciously. And if I ever do, please do not hesitate to let me know because that would break my heart. I am a man who needs a woman with the intuition feelings and emotions and love and of faith in God that will bring us to the heights of heaven together. Beyond the stars. Only if you feel like it, and if the timing is right, God willing.

I will be on the computer at 5 pm waiting anxiously for you, and if you should not make it for one reason or another, I will undoubtedly understand, God bless with love and prayers, to my wife Ginette from your husband, Thomas.

I love. You, honey, did I mention to you that I love you?

Maybe I forgot, I love you, smile. The time right now is 7:55 am.

We got it, Dr., and I honestly have the faith God willing I feel spiritually it's going to happen. We are going to have children, and we are going to see our grandchildren.

Please understand that I have been living alone for 4 years, waiting for you patiently, and I have talked to thousands of other ladies who have always tried to Scam me. Or want me to send them money, and I pray you to understand that I am a little skeptical, and I should not. We had talked together too long and communicated to long in a way that only God would want to be together.

Sometimes I am not real bright, so please give me a kick in the pants and let me know when I'm not the sharpest tool in the shed. Smile. God, I love this woman: you are so precious in understanding, and when you let me know you understand when I feel most ladies would fly off the handle and get upset. Although not my wife, she is so understanding, honest, trusting, and a guardian angel of love in my heart. Could have only came from heaven. I have hurt your feelings and you have broken my heart.

April 27, 2018

Thomas:

I feel a lady doctor would have more compassion for me and our situation than a man. I still have your phone number: she may want to call you and talk to you.

Another thing that occurred to me whenever you tell someone you have met somebody online, especially men. Encountering a lady and let the doctor know that we have met in person. What do you think? It doesn't matter to me, my love. You the one who inspired me, and I'm Looking. I have always felt spiritual that it was against God's law, I do care about you, and I care about your family and my love for you.

Sweetheart, I have to go pick up some medication for Frank, who lives out in the guesthouse. The friend of his that has a limousine service is going to show us a great time and all the great sites. I have to meet with him in a half-hour, so I am going to drive right now to make sure Frank has his medication. I love you, God bless you, and may your beautiful heavenly spirit show brightly tonight in heaven, and I love you.

You have good Friday night sweetheart, my prayers are with you, and whatever you do have fun and be free. Let me know if you want me to write you another story? I enjoy writing to them about you, and I think I might write this evening. I was reasonably selfish in the last stories I wrote, and I thought this one is for you, sweetheart.

If you would like for me not to write to you any more stories of the context I was writing, I will not. I love you, and you are worth it, and God loves you. How about if I write a story about the two of us? Our love and leave out the love content unless you so desire it. It depends on the mood we're in, and sometimes it's appropriate, and sometimes we don't feel like it. And I understand, so please let me know, sweetheart.

I'm so excited about talking to this female doctor. I just have a feeling God is going to be with us let us pray together so we can stay together. I love you.

April 28, 2018

Thomas wrote:

Did I mention to you that I love you today, and every day after that? I think of you and our love.

Check your yahoo email let me know when you receive the books please, I love you and miss you.

April 29, 2018

Thomas wrote:

How was your day? God be with you.

Your husband, to my beautiful lovely wife, my God-loving wife, my God-fearing wife, and her God-fearing husband.

> *How are you today, sweetheart? I pray you are doing well and have a good weekend, God bless with love and prayers Thomas.*

April 30, 2018

Ginette wrote:

> *Good morning my love, you've been forever, and it's good when someone realizes when they do wrong. I am okay with the name Ginette! It makes me would cause me to think you're still searching online to hook up with ladies. And that you shouldn't be taken seriously as you just Ginette pass time online. I'm glad that you were finally able to get hold of a Doctor, especially a female, so that it will be fine. I'll wait for her call, and yes I'll let her know we have met in person,*
>
> *I don't understand why people are so fast to stick their noses in other people's matters. I don't blame them too, and it is due to some dishonest people. Out of a hundred percent, you may have that 1 or 2% that is so, no matter what, there are still good people in this world. I pray that the happiness we both wants will come to the past and that God will surely bless us. Nothing can change me from loving you, my love, and I hope you think the same as well. You enjoy the rest of your day till we chat again soon. Yes, I got your lovely messages via email, and thanks so much, you're such a romantic person Thomas. Kisses, I'll lie down and will wake up for work later.*

MAY 2018, ROMANTIC MEMOIRS FROM HEAVEN

Ginette 1 May 2018,

Hi, my love, not sure you're here. Hi again.

Thomas 1 May 2018,

I am now. How is my beautiful Angel wife doing? I cannot stop thinking about you and living a life together with you. You are so precious, and I was sleeping. I apologize so that I will be at the computer for quite some time. I will look forward to chatting with you when you get the opportunity at your convenience. God loves and us: I love you and miss you. Or do I miss you and love you? Yes, I. think that's it. I miss you so much.

I went to bed at 1. AM in the morning, a friend of mine showed up at noon today and woke me. Did you get that CD slideshow that I email you? You're tired and more than likely sleeping. I wish we were laying together holding each other one day, have a good. A Night with love and prayers, sweetheart, and do not forget to say your prayers because God loves you, and I love you.

Ginette

Hi Thomas

Ginette, how are you, my sweet angel? I love you for who you are. You are a Christian lady who is worth compassion, trust, and love. That God has endowed, through me for you. Is anything you need or anything I can do for you? We keep missing each other for a reason, and it makes me think about you more.

Are you still awake, my love? I keep falling asleep and waking up.

Thomas 2 May

Yes, I am, sweetheart, are you? You are always on my mind. You still will be On my mind. I love you to call me on the telephone, and if I hear one ring, I will know to come here and chat with you. I have a bell turned on that if you come on to the computer, I am Right here, and it is quiet. Let me know if you would like me to write you a Romance story? I'm not sure if you want romance?

I do so enjoy writing them to you, and I not only miss you, I wish you were here so we can love each other. I cannot quit thinking about you, and I never will. Because you are the soulmate that I prayed for, and on some level, you prayed for the same thing, a soulmate. A Christian soulmate equally yoked. A beautiful lady, a nice looking gentleman with great intentions for our future together, helping others. By setting the example through the Holy Spirit and the grace of God, something scarce spiritually. I just want you here in my arm, holding you, talking to you, and having fun together and trusting love, a precious commodity and characteristic nowadays.

We will always feel that way about each other because we are willing to grow along spiritual lines. Love your name, especially when it came to the Bible. I'm going to lie down now, and please call me anytime at 24 seven: if it rings once, I will check and see if you are here if I'm not sleeping. I love you. I miss you, and God loves both of us. Jesus is coming like a thief in the night, and gracious things are happening, like you.

Together through the grace of God to help many souls, God commenced our spiritual soulmate and friendship. Well, why not? Waiting is a waste of life: where's my sweet, beautiful wife? I love you, and I miss you. What do you tell your girlfriends about You and me? Anything or everything? I have been revealing more and more people, the spirit working through me. Just a few friends that the spirit speaks through me. Feeling a need to let everyone know, or certain people, how much I miss you and love you.

Thomas

Yesterday, 3:42 am

Why can't I stop thinking about my wife? Is it because I love her and want to perform miracles for hundreds of souls, if not thousands and thousands? I know God put us together for that reason: things are happening for the right people. Are you changing for the bad and good? I love you.

I pray you are doing well today, sweetheart: I cannot stop thinking about you.

Pres. Donald Trump, his wife, there is a 24 year age difference. Dr. Phil and his wife, there is a 34 year age difference. We can do this. The key to love is understanding spoken words and actions, little things that say so much: the access to love is forgiveness, accepting our mistakes. Not forgetting, by remembering to cut ourselves some breaks. Love is sharing fortunes and bad: facing things together will wipe away what is sad.

Love is giving free, and with your heart, without the thought of return. That's where love respects each other's differences and views, together with the common bond — inspiring each other's joy. Laughter will be inside of us, and patience unlocks the door learning with respect: the little things we are never too old to hold hands, and we must remember to say, I love you at least once a day, and never go to sleep angry.

Love is never taking the other for granted, and It should come through all the years that we love each other together. Love is standing together, facing the world, and forming a circle of love. Family love is doing things for each other, the spirit of joy with the grace of God. Love is speaking words of appreciation and gratitude in thoughtful ways. It is not expecting the husband to wear a halo or the wife to have an angel's wings. Love does not look for perfection in each other, and it is cultivating together with love and growing along spiritual lines.

Love is having an understanding and a sense of humor, having the capacity to forgive and forget. Love is giving each other in which each can grow. Love is of the spirit and is reciprocal: love is not only marrying the right partner: love is being with the right partner.

But we will also begin to understand that love is more than verses on valentines and romance in the movies: we start to know that love is here and now, real and genuine. The essential thing in our lives for love is the creator of our favorite memories and the foundation of our fondest dreams. Love is a promise that is always kept, and love is a fortune never to be spent. A seed that can flourish, and even the most unlikely of places. In this radiance that never fades, this mysterious and magical joy is only known by those who love, from the grace of God. so ignore the mistakes, you are not perfect, and the passion for romance is perfection's thoughts and feelings.

And I merged in a romantic moment which gives me at last, you around me for once, you beneath me, above me, love in you, like me may linger, my sweet, beautiful love. The moment is eternal, and there is no more anything but love eternally, between you, and I love you.

And made love ecstasies together, we will be forever happy, joyous and free. It will be a love we may love, on and into eternity.

True love is a sacred flame, That burns eternally between you and me, and true destiny love speaks, and with gentle true love gives with open-heart. True love conquers, makes no harsh commands, and neither rules nor binds. And true love holds our hearts love, our marriage and love desire love, is a bond known.

Although our love comes from and is taken to heaven, love has no time for fools. I have never written to anyone that I have a pet like you. You shall not walk alone, and my heart will be yours. Your home is more beautiful than roses.

Love is more beautiful than a dream, a bond between two hearts. When we love, the time spent apart sharing common interests working through all fears looking at ourselves. As if two were in the mirror, we will find common ground together.

On issues not agreed to give into arguments being tender to all your needs, Ginette, I will be there forever, and always all I want to do is to hold you forever. Love me when you are bored, love me as you always have loved me. With compassion for yourself, through the Holy Spirit and Jesus Christ.

I will be there for your loneliness, and together we will love and never come apart from our hearts.

I will love you forever, God surrounding you, and my love is spiritual, precious, and sweet.

I want to grow old with you: I want to make you smile whenever you're sad, I will grow in love with you. I want to make you smile and grow in love together forever.

God loves you with the love of John chapter 3, verse 16: love is like magic. Miraculous, there is nothing in life that our love cannot change. Love can transform the most commonplace into a beautiful place.

Our love is unselfish for each other, and our passion is kind: our love sees with its heart and not with its mind. Loves the answer that everyone seeks, love is priceless, and free may include our love last forever. We will love each other as one love, and if we must separate ways, my passion remains with you: you have my heart.

You know I love you: I will be with you. I love you, not only for what you have made of yourself, what you're going to be making of me. Your love is a part of me that will bring out the love I have for you.

My love, the love I have for you is beautiful that no one else can see. And my passion has done it by being yourself. Love is what being married means, after all.

Somewhere there within is our love and the desire for another lonely soul. How can I compare you for your more lovely, and our passion is shining from heaven.

Our love is God's, and every angel will guide us along with the miracles. It makes me want to love you even more, and you know that, of course, when we get married. It is a marriage, a journey: you are the right lady. We will have to learn together how to share on many different levels. Talking from the heart and praying together is not far apart: this is how much I cannot take my mind off you.

I love you: you are a precious gift from God, a miracle through the grace of God and Jesus Christ, our Lord. I miss you and have fun writing to you, which makes my heart jump for joy and a fire that I have never had or even experienced. God spiritually joined us: you are my miracle, and you are my girl, and when we finally meet, my smile will go from cheek to cheek.

I have to leave for now to take Frank shopping, it's 1 pm, and I pray to get back to chat. I have been with you all morning, all day, since I woke you are with me. During the night, you gave me that burning light of love that I miss, and I will provide you with a French kiss when we're married. I will love you like kissing a cherry, bless with love and prayers, your husband, Thomas. I love you. I'm thinking about you. I'm going to love you the way you like to be enjoyed, from the spirit above.

Ginette

> Good afternoon my love, we have missed each other so much on here, and honestly, I wouldn't say I like the feeling of having to miss you when you take so much of your time to send me such a lengthy message. As sad as it is, I know we are never out of each other's hearts and minds. You're on my mind all the time! Kisses and hugs.

Thomas

> I'm here at 12:50 pm, Ginette. I love you and miss you. I know better than to eat Chinese food had me down for a couple of days. Although I do enjoy eating it and forget about the after- effects, LOL I love you.

> The post office is closed here right now for one hour for lunch. I will call them in another hour: you're my beautiful angel, and I. pray to God. God sends me the most precious angel beyond my imagination, and I thank God through Jesus Christ, our Lord's name, for having you in my life.

> It's because of you, I have learned how to love and am growing spiritually in love. We have for one another one day to together forever, kiss and hugs and a lot more from me, smile you bring the joy for living and giving to my life, for the rest of my life, one day possible to be my wife.

> I love you and miss you, wish you were here, wish I was there, wish we were together, anywhere. Smile. I also sent them to your email address. I apologize once again for missing each other, and I will be on at 5.:00 PM possibly a little before, see if we can touch bases. I love you.

Ginette

> Hello, I just woke up. I'm sorry, I wait for you.

Thomas

> I pray that you realize, of course, you are a Christian and have been saved as we have. My priority in a relationship, although if you find another man, a young Christian

man, we will always be friends, and we will always love one another. And I pray to God as I prayed for you, unexpected, of course. I must let that love go and be free, meant to be it will come back: if not, I will certainly see you in heaven or be with you. I do not want you to feel obligated or committed, so please live your life freely and know that you have a friend that loves and cares about you. You have done a lot for me, and I cannot thank you enough outside of meeting you. Which was like Christmas morning, and I will never forget you: I will always think about you. I just wanted you to be free and not be upset with me. Life is too short to wait, and waiting is a waste of energy.

Please do not feel guilty if you find an excellent young preacher and man who will take care of you. The way we have chatted together, I would want you to expect the same for you. As I feel towards us, someone with compassion and love, and trust will love you and take care of you. Let us turn our will and our lives over the responsibility of God and pray like I'm sure you and I both do. We love God with all our hearts through Jesus Christ, our Lord's name: you will always be a love that I will always love with Christ in our life. The book of John 3: 16.

I will always love you no matter who you are with or where you are, and I will be here for you when you need me. We are both from the future because we have faith and love. God gave us the rainbow promised Noah that he would never flood the earth again. Jesus is coming like a thief in the night. We know not when. The year 2018 of our Lord, if we get called home and only have one friend, we are very fortunate. Someone that loves us has compassion for us. That can be trusted and trusted through Jesus Christ, our Lord's name. I pray for Ginette that

she has no worry or concern: things will flow easily in her life because she is worth it. God loves her if we have to struggle with the chaos that is not God's way for Christians: the spirit should flow smoothly without fear. Love for the one you love: recall that the crow was sent out from Noah's Ark never came back when the dove sent out. It came back with an olive branch.

One thing we will always do is always remember you. You will never forget me because together, we change each other for the better. Through the discernment of the Holy Spirit, we were touched and still are and always will be protected. We will always be there to protect one another through the Holy Spirit in Jesus Christ, our Lord's name.

I will never pull out our love for one another 24 seven. You can cuddle with me because I love you. I will always be with you no matter who you're with, what you are doing, through the discernment of God. Because you have touched my life and a spiritual way, everyone needs love from above.

I Prayed, and I devote my life to God and service, thank you, God, for Ginette in my life. And we both know we will be in each other's lives forever and eternally. And it's a precious love that you cannot recapture, never forgotten, always remembered ever. Thank you, God. Jesus gave his life for us, and who should, howsoever, believe in Him, will not perish but have everlasting life.

Time stops at the speed of light: 1000 years is one day for God: heaven is only 1500 mi.[2]. However, another dimension has been mentioned twice in the Lord's prayer. Matthew 6: 9- 14, Jesus is not a liar entered into this world as God in the flesh to save us. For that, I thank God for Ginette in my life: it is incredible and miraculous to me that God would set Ginette into my life at the right time and the right place. An answer to my prayer far beyond my comprehension.

The discernment and the Holy Spirit is working through me of a love that a man and a woman should cherish. And should always have in their life, so much in the respect that they walk in the light of God.

Ginette, I'm going to work on another project writing a letter to the Veterans Administration at the Pentagon in Washington, DC. Suppose the treatment of veterans happens not to change. They have doctors and nurses, and we have to wait for hours. I do not wait for anything. They do not like to see me coming because they know me: I'm looking at World War II veterans, Korean War veterans, Vietnam veterans, and Gulf War veterans. When I walk into the newest Veterans Administration hospital in the world, they know I have arrived because I will help other veterans.

And the devil would be proud of my language, smile anyway I raise Cain and rightfully so like when Jesus walked into the father's temple. Using it for a flea market, Jesus was not happy.

Please let me know if you got the control numbers for the books that were sent to you. Like I had mentioned earlier, the only thing I could imagine is that the coins on the bookmarks they would reject.

I will always love you. Sweetheart, feel free to fly and live your life okay. Take a breath of air and relax and be my beautiful. And we know we will always love Jesus Christ, our Lord, as Christians. *The first time he came as a lamb, the next time he comes, it will be like a roaring lion, will not be happy.*

I lost count of the funeral services I have attended recently. Two more coming up, something will have to do a celebration of life. 11 Corinthians 5: 8 – To be absent from the flesh is to be present with the Lord. If you feel suffocated or obligated or guilty in any way, keep in mind I am a writer. That's what I love to do.

I find my writing and writing can help others, as I have mentioned before. I'm writing music in between. I love to write music and lyrics. So far, I have loved the way we have loved one another. Do you have any issues? Other than can we not get together on our timing for chatting?

I realize I must be frustrating for you. I fell asleep I was going to take a nap at 4 pm our time, awaken at 5:35 pm. I have to accept responsibility for my actions, and I do not want you to consider that. I have to pray everything happens for a reason, and I miss you. I love you, a huge hug for you and a French kiss for hours, and a smile would like you to be free from me for a while. Because I am a chatterbox smile, we will connect, God's time, not ours: please do not get frustrated or feel obligated once again. Go free, have fun, and be God's precious child, happy, joyous, and free. I could sit here. And write to you for hours.

Then you would have to read it all the time halfway through: you would be so upset with me. Sometimes the least amount said has the most impact of meaning. Have a good night. God bless with love and prayers, Thomas.

Quite a bit of editing would have to be done to be Christianity. In the light of God's eyes, we can do this: we are doing this, it will help many people save a lot of souls. God would approve of, and Jesus Christ, the Lord's name.

Would you like me to Start on the album? I know you have mentioned you wanted to wait and do it together? I'm going to lay down for a little while. I'll be back in about an hour.

I pray, God willing. Ginette, check your Yahoo email, please? Thank you. Have a good evening. I'm going to. Bed tries to catch up with you tomorrow, not sure you got this: let me know what you think?

Ginette,

Good morning my love, Thomas: sorry, I was so tired last night and wouldn't sign on yahoo. I'm very sorry about that. I just woke up not too long and thought to check on here for you. I see a long message full of emotions and love, and I feel you have made my day.

You're right: saving a soul is something one can do without even knowing that person. Godly words would also protect a whole population, and I'm interested in doing that to be a part of such remarkable work of God. I have a few Christian pen pals that I have known for sometimes who are poor and living in distress, and it would be a blessing for them to read what we have to offer in our books. I realize God brought us together for a higher purpose, and we will have to allow ourselves to be used by Him.

For me, I see you as a lover, a teacher, and best friend, and I know that's what God wants in a relationship.

Oh, honey, you're relaxed, and I don't know who will be that guy that would be full of love the way you do. I have no one in mind apart from you, and no matter what, always know, the bond between you and I wouldn't be shaken by anyone or anything. Rest assured that I'm yours forever, and you're mine even in heaven.

You're such a kind person and a real soldier that stands for his right. You're not selfish because you stand for the welfare of your colleagues: that's so amazing, my love. I know with you I'll be protected. I try to let you know anything, and I'll get ready to go now: I guess you're still asleep dreaming about us!

Thomas

I'm here, sweetheart: my apology once again I spent time writing to You and thinking about you: I want our love for each other to be free, and that I do not want you to feel obligated. I want you to have fun, and possibly love will come your way. That's what I pray. I know our love will be together again in heaven with God.

I want to be with you, but that's what I want, and I like the best for you: I want you to be happy, joyous, and free I love you.

Ginette

Hey, honey, I'm here!

It's 11:30, and I'm still awake hope you're still here.

Thomas

Hi Ginette, I have imagined today that I love you. You're going to have a good book, and I feel your picture on the front cover would be phenomenal. Will teach through the spirit of God and the Holy Spirit how to come back to Christianity as couples and live a happy, joyous life together forever in eternity.

God answered my prayer when he sent you to me, putting us along on a mission to save a lot of souls. We are so fortunate to have been chosen as God's elect, everything happens for a reason, and we will help others: God knows our hearts.

He knows that we came into this world with nothing, and we will leave the same way, although He will allow us to help not only ourselves but also many others.

I would not like you to feel obligated or guilty or resentment or regrets in this relationship. God may have something else in mind for you, but at present, you have changed my life.

For that, I thank God through Jesus Christ Lord's name. You are such a precious angel, and when I get to heaven, and God asked me why I did not take care of one of His angels? What am I going to say? That's how I feel about you: let us pray together that we may stay together, a bond of God remains in our spirit working to help other people.

Blasphemy of the Holy Spirit is the only unforgiven sin, and that is when you do not let the Holy Spirit work through you to teach others the truth. It may not be what they want to hear, but the truth is God of love.

We will take one moment in time and live our lives to the happiness and joy in the miraculous gift we have been given through the grace of God. I pray for you. I waited for you for 16 years, and God shall be a surprise like Christmas morning.

I was a little shocked at our age difference, although you have shown me that you are very mature and well educated through our communication. And we are spiritually yoked, with God through Jesus Christ, our Lord, we devote our lives to God and service.

Thomas

Ginette, I pray you had a good day: it was undoubtedly exciting chatting with you over lunch. I'm just curious, so do not get excited, please, the smile. I'm not sure I understand why you're looking for an apartment? When you have a home waiting for you, together, God is going to take care of us, and we will be secured.

How long have you lived in Canada? Another question do you speak another language? These are assets because I care, and I inquire because I care.

I was targeting a young lady, beautiful, such as yourself, marketing the books. And it would take that nice-looking young lady that would be promoting two great books. That can teach others, and save many souls, so we are not alone on this project: God is working with us.

I am working on the second book "Soul Sanctuary" for mistakes and additions, and you're an additional asset to the reader.

I pray we can touch bases, and you're not too tired. If you are, we can contact you at a later point in time. You know I love you, Ginette, and care about you with compassion, trust.

Through the grace of God, because you're worth it, I'm equally as pleased with your picture. And believing you need to be romanced with enthusiasm, joyful anticipation, and excitement with the compassion that is on fire, mmm.

I lost your phone number or, put it this way, I put it in a safe place, and I cannot find it for the life of my smile.

From these three verses in Luke, the following is known of Anna: She was a prophetess.

Luke 2:36–38 There was also a prophet, Anna, the daughter of Phanuel, of Asher's tribe. She was very old: she had lived with her husband seven years after her marriage and then was a widow until she was eighty-four.[*] She never left the temple but *worshiped night and day, fasting and praying. Coming up to them at that very moment, she gave thanks to God and spoke about the child to all who were looking forward to the redemption of Jerusalem.*

Ginette

Yes, I can't complain too much one must be strong.

Thomas

We are blessed that God has a purpose for us. It's almost surreal the love we have for each other and that God has for us.

Ginette

Yeah.

Thomas

Get some rest, sweetheart, my beautiful lovely lady, I do not want to let you go, but I want you to be happy. And you need to get some rest. I love you so much and think about you continuously, and it is so much more that we. are going to add together.

Ginette

Okay, I'll go to bed now, and I'm relieved since we have chatted love you so much, and sweet dreams. You're in my heart and prayers.

Thomas

I'm excited that we have finally connected. Good night sweetheart, I love you. I miss you, and I think of you. God bless with love and prayers. Do not forget to say your prayers.

Ginette

Thomas

My love, my soulmate, together with saving souls, few questions beautiful, I cannot find your phone number.

Being a woman, I feel she will have more compassion for the two of us online: we met on a Christian site, and that we have been communicating for quite some time now. And that you have not asked me for one penny, and are you available for a telephone call at the time of my appointment? Just in case, and I thank you, my precious love, who needs to be French kissed for hours.

Inspired to attend a good friend of mine's funeral service, I believe I sent you a picture of him and his wife? Bonnie and Clyde, the 10 June, my love.

Can I write you a romantic love letter? I'm in the mood anytime you are: God willing, let me know, sweetheart. I love you, miss you, and would like to be with you together, partner, and wife. I love you forever. I would like for you to let me know when you think you can come to our home. I have no one else, and God put us together for that reason. I could think of nothing better than my wife.

I cannot stop thinking about you, through the grace of God, the feelings I have for you spiritually. I feel that they are from God through Jesus Christ, our Lord. When I get to heaven, and God asked me, "why did I not take care of one of his precious angels"? I would like to say I have loved this angel with compassion through the Holy Spirit and Jesus Christ, our Lord's name.

And I pray every day, and we can do very well together. I do not have anyone to help promote books, and I love to write. I have six books written, not edited.

I wish you were here to help me, and then I want to hurry back home and be with your friends and mother. Then come back down here, see me, and be together. And then go back, and come back, go back, come back, smile. I love you, and possibly that can happen, God willing. God will provide for us. He knows we would like to help other people. If there's anything I can do or anything you need, please let me know: I love you.

Darling sweetheart Angel, delicious, tasty kiss, how are you? I pray you had a good weekend Ginette: my prayers are always with you, and miracles do happen. If you have faith, God placed us together for a reason. I've been to business all my life. I know correctly what to do: all I need is a beautiful young lady such as yourself. My wife, I do not have much now: I have working hard for our future. Did you receive the books yet? It is a piece of gold waiting to be joined in our bedchamber, shared with care and compassion.

I have some lady from Nigeria, just sent me a text stating that she was getting her father's fortune and that she's from Norfork, Virginia. And I told her I'd heard that line before, and we don't have much.

Am I assuming you do have a driver's license?

Be out and about in two months, and there will be a lot to do to promote and work together on this project. And it will be fun, and we will enjoy each other's company immensely: you are perfect. These are all God's thoughts. All we have to do is have faith and pray because faith without works is dead. You can work when you want to, as many hours as you care to: there will be no clock, and even take a day or two off of work, if we care.

Think about it sweetheart, seriously, the sooner we get started on this project with the grace of God, we will be stable. I am optimistic: my faith is unshakable.

I have experienced miracles, a biblical proportion that I have written in the book, and my beautiful sweet young lovely scrumptious wife is an angel. That only God could have sent for this miracle to proceed. Let me know as soon as possible what you think about it? And when you can come to Arizona and get started. With the life that you will never want, and we will have financial stability. So you can travel back and forth, if you care to, as I have mentioned. I have been in business all my life, and I know the ins and outs. I do know how to negotiate.

Well, sweetheart, I'm going to bed right now: you're more than likely asleep. I pray you had fun this weekend and a good weekend: it is 11:10 pm here. God bless with love and prayers, have a good day or night. Hugs and French kisses, Thomas.

Just dreaming about you, or I should say us. I feel that you would be feeling trapped to make a commitment like marriage right off the bat. Why don't we take our time, see what's a convenient time for you, to come down here, and we won't get married? Not right away anyway, I would be nervous about having some guy I never met before, wanted to get married right off. That would make me feel uncomfortable, and as I have stated, it's about you being happy, or I should say us being happy together.

I would still love for you to come down and move right into our home, take it slow and see other things go. I'm sure God will forgive us: that's why Jesus died on the cross, it will be like a vacation for you. And see how compatible we are when we get together. If we are not happy with one another and find out we are not, it would be a mistake to get married. I need your feedback on this, or I would like your input on this.

Let us both pray to God through the grace of Jesus Christ, our Lord. That we are both happy with one another, and I will treat you with compassion, consideration, love, trust, honor, and code between us, a spiritual bond.

I love you because I do. I love you for the beautiful young lady you are. And let us grow along spiritual lines and do the right thing. It is 3 am right now, I went to sleep for a little while, and I woke up, and I prayed. To God about the situation, and these are some options that we can take into consideration.

I just want you to be happy, so think about what I have written, and we will consider it to be in business together.

You will get a feel for who I am, their kind of autobiography, and how much I do love God, Jesus Christ, our Lord, and the Holy Spirit. We pray too that moves throughout the earth, answering prayers. One of the gifts that Jesus left us, Jesus, also left us the power to cast out evil spirits in his name: all you have to do is yell or say the word Jesus, please help me. And whatever evil spirit is bothering you will instantly crouch down and back away. Jesus also left us with the power of hands-on healing.

Three gifts Jesus left us, along with the salvation of our sins. He died on the cross for us: it hurts my heart and brings tears to my heart. A God so powerful would give his life for us. God loves us that much, we are his creation, and He wants the best for us, and we want the best.

I feel we will create a specific situation for both of us: neither of us will have to want. So you will be able to go back and forth between Arizona and Canada. And if it means getting married to get United States citizenship, to be able to travel, back and forth. We will get married, and we will write up our contract, as God as our mediator.

I am an ordained minister, and I feel there would be nothing wrong with your husband being married to his wife legally. We may have to get married, and I'm not sure of citizenship circumstances in the United States. You will have to check on that one yourself, or you may know more about it than I do.

I want you to relax, feel comfortable, be happy, and please do not worry or have any opposing thoughts about anything. Whatever you want to do, I'm in total agreement with the love, trust, compassion from my heart and soul. God bless with love, and prayers, your business partner, your friend, your husband.

A man you could feel trust with and comfortable with. I love to laugh and have fun, Thomas. Have a good day, sweetheart, or good night. Another option, if you feel more comfortable, is bringing a friend with you. You're more than welcome to do that, and we do have options and consideration for one another. Anything you can think of, sweetheart, to make you happy and comfortable. With the grace of God, should be our primary goal, let us pray.

It appears that the second book "Soul Sanctuary" will be out within the month. I emailed you this letter I received from the publisher and editorial department of the publishing company. A memoir also serves as a resource for those in the throes of addiction to change their ways by coming to God.

You cover a great deal of ground in this work, sharing many parts of your life. Offering hope and guidance and seeking to encourage and teach. Others who once faced or are currently facing challenges, such as poverty, rape, domestic abuse, and drug and alcohol abuse. Also included is a description of your time in the Marines, which is interesting to read. Soul Sanctuary is a multifaceted autobiography that ultimately bears testimony that one's life can be entirely changed for the better after a long run of misfortune and trauma.

We have decisions to make concerning and considering the third book. I have five books outlined and a miraculous communion between two spiritual people that are equally yoked with God.

I'm sure you understand, and I have a lot of work to do working with the editorial department going through the whole book, "Soul Sanctuary." They are giving me a two-week deadline. God bless Thomas. God will enfold to us our destiny when the time is right, and we will always remain friends, you and I both know.

Ginette wrote:

One more time, this is funny became semi-back to me, I pray to God. 'Hello Thomas'

Feb and June 2018. On yahoo messenger.

Ginette

Hi, my love.

Hello honey, sorry I missed you last night: I waited for a while but then I fell asleep, and this morning I saw your sweet message. It's always good to hear from you, I got the package this morning and was so excited about that, and I'll try to take a look at those and take a few pictures so you know I got it. Thanks so much for all your prayers and kind messages. I'll check back later to chat with you. Enjoy the rest of your day till then. Your sweetheart Ginette.

Thomas

I'm going to lay down for a little while, and get back up, and work on the book. Honorable mention to my sweetheart, the love of my life, for the rest of our life. I cannot imagine a life without you: now that I met you, my heart wants to be with you.

I'm leaving for, town in a few minutes: get some gasoline and a haircut, God willing. I will talk to you this evening or later on today. Please leave a message, sweetheart, and God bless with love and prayers, Thomas. Ginette, I'm available, and I will keep checking from time to time. I love you, and God loves you.

Ginette

Ginette shared a photo.

Thomas 8 May 2018,

I hope your day. Was beautiful.

With hugs and kisses, going to lay down for a little while, I love you.

Ginette

Hey Thomas

Not sure you're still here: I'll be here a little: I'm falling asleep so tired tonight.

Ginette wrote: 25 May 2018

Good morning my love: I hope you had a great day yesterday and also a great night's sleep. Sorry, I was not able to message you yesterday. I was so exhausted and decided to write to you this morning since it's Saturday. No work today, so I'll get some rest, but I thought to message you first before starting my day.

Thanks for understanding my explanation. It's not my intention to ever bring misunderstanding. I believe we have passed that stage, and we were going along well, and I don't want anything to ruin our relationship. So thanks for understanding, and know that you're also forgiven.

I promise to always have a forgiven heart for you. You're so right: whether a person is illiterate, no one notices their limitations once they have manners. Styles are not earned quickly because they must be natural and not something you copy just for the time being. It is like receiving salvation: you don't receive it with pretense but must only be inherent in your heart.

Thanks for elaborating on manners: all you mentioned is just the facts, and I can't argue that. Yes, I remembered when we first met, and I told her about you, and she respects him. I think it was the start of me considering you, and because God has been with us, here we are. God uses my Mom to establish this between us. I know God is going to help us and make us one small United family.

I see Boyd as someone for us to show love and care for him because God brought him your way to be of great help to you. And after we come to be a help to us all, in life when somebody understands you better it useful to show them, love. Boyd is closer to you than anyone right now. We will always love, care, and respect him.

I think God is putting things in place: we only need to continue prayers, and everything will get in the right place. Give news on how it's all went. I'll try to get some rest and get out there later. Thanks so much for your message and all the news. I'll give you an update on my traveling arrangements as soon as I hear anything. Enjoy the rest of your day. All my love to you. Warm kisses and hugs from your northern girl.

JUNE 2018, ROMANTIC MEMOIRS FROM HEAVEN

Thomas wrote: 7 Jun 2018.

I want to spend 5 to 10 minutes at least speaking with you on the telephone. And if you would be so kind as to give me your telephone number, I would call you at a specific time. I had mentioned before, and I pray this does not sound like I am trying to control you. I'm sure you can understand the reason why I would recommend this suggestion.

And many ingredients go into the cake before we place the cherry on top, do you not agree?

We must become friends first, okay? I love you and care about you. God loves us because we are Christians: you realize you can tell me anything.

If you have time to put into a relationship, and the other party is putting everything into this relationship.

I will be checking this Yahoo messenger for your answer and reply.

I am a Christian: you are right: you say you are a Christian. I pray you can understand what I am saying? This does not mean I don't care about you or do not love you. As you can tell from my communication, I do like you. I do care about you, and I do want to bond together one day. As of God's precious children bonded and love with one another through the grace of God. And if you feel that is not going to happen, please be honest with me and let me know what kind of relationship you think we have?

Please let me know so that I can consider our friendship and relationship, which is just pen-pals who write to each other once in a while online. I will slack off on my communication with you, and we will talk from time to time because I care about you.

You are worth it, although I'm not going to build on that kind of a relationship. And I'm sure you can understand that, so the decision is yours. I would be more than happy to share with you. God blessed with love and prayers, Thomas.

Ginette wrote: 8 Jun

Good morning my love. I hope you had a great night. Not sure you're still awake yet, so let me respond to your messages.

I don't speak on the phone: first, English is my second language, and French my first. I do well in writing than verbally, so I'm mostly shy, but I still try not to be nervous because communication is essential in any relationship.

Sometimes due to work, I get tired, so you notice I don't chat much, and you do mostly ask me to get rest, you also ask me to go to bed, so what's the big deal here, my love?

My Mom does not live closer, and where I am now is closer to work, so if I move back, I would not be able to get to on time and would end up losing it. I hope you understand.

I understand all you're saying: forgive me if I sound harsh, but I'm not. We started communication till now we had ups and downs. You know I do my best to put in the time to communicate with you.

I read your books, and I'm still doing that, you write so much, Thomas, and I have to make time to read it all carefully. But with my pace.

You have a good day, and I'll get ready now. No matter what you think about it, I still love and respect you. Ginette.

Ginette wrote:

Hi, my love,

I just wrote you a message on yahoo messenger. The address down is what you should use because it's the house address I gave you when you sent the package,

You started doubting from the onset, so I'm not surprised at all with all that is going on. Enjoy your night. I have to sleep now. Your wife to be. Friends missing each other since I last messaged you today. I was at work by then, so sorry I was not checking my email or yahoo messenger frequently.

I'm not angry at all and sometimes understand how people take things. In life, it is only with trust that people can conquer the world. The number there is my old number: that was when I was in Calgary. I'll go to bed now. Have a sweet one.

Thomas wrote: 9 Jun

So simple, according to your selfish male friend, why on God's green earth is he not giving?. According to him, I do not need all the ups and downs. Your male friend started doubting from the onset: according to your male friend, I must be an idiot: this is comical. I know the difference between how a man thinks and talks that a lady, this was not you talking or your friend was not a female either. So you're not surprised at all with all that is going on.

I would have told him to mind his own business and disowned him as a friend giving you that kind of advice: of course, you may have a relationship going with him, and I would be okay. I would be happy for you Ginette, I love you, God bless, and I miss you, have a good day.

Ginette wrote: 11 Jun

Hi honey,

Sorry, I fell asleep and just realize I didn't send the information. I'm not trying to understand your suggestions, but we did already talked and then another idea. Coming to Arizona is also essential to me, but I said I can't be homeless now and pack up to travel like I was telling you earlier. Coming isn't just getting on the plane. I'm leaving another country to remember. My Mom and I must sit and talk and decide on things, and there are a few things that I need to consider before traveling. Arizona isn't downtown Montreal my love.

I have prayed and asked God to make you understand. As long as we are happy and getting along, we will do better when we start to live together. My Mom's health isn't in good shape, and I can't just leave her like that one thing to consider. She may live with us if I must go to the US. I truly understand the need for us to work together for writing and not just that life together. Life is short, and I know the need to be with someone that loves you and cares.

Since we met, your concern and care can never be forgotten, and my only wish is for us not to be fighting. I realize we have been doing that for the last time, and it's not right for you or me. Please think about me and how important to have a place. This way, I can better plan to travel. Have a great night, honey. I have to go back to bed very tired. Hugs and kisses.

Thomas wrote: 18 Jun

To my sweet little lovely Ginette is even more to our heart. I have been honest as I can with you, and I felt everything. I tell you everything also send you an autobiography about my past life.

If what your mother said to you is correct, you have one of the greatest spiritual precious mothers with wisdom and knowledge beyond my comprehension. Please let your mother know how I feel about her and that what she had said to you in your conversation about me to her, as an outsider looking in.

I have just witnessed and heard, or should I say, read the greatest mother on this planet.

Love and kisses.

Ginette wrote: 20 Jun

Good morning Thomas,

I have been getting all your messages, and I like to tell you that I'm not trying to ignore you: it's not my style. I'm a very respectful person.

I'm also glad that there's a possibility that you can still make children: I'm proud and almost felt guilty for pushing you away. I honestly love you more than you know. I would be excited to have kids with someone that loves, respect, and care for me, and you remember I told you I didn't get these from my previous relationship.

My Mom and I discussed you and me concerning visiting you: though she's afraid and concern about my security, she encouraged me to see you for a week, so as I pray and thought sincerely, I want to give it a try.

So I'll ask for an excuse for a week from work and see my Mom. My Mom lives in Calgary, so after that, I'll get my ticket. Have a beautiful morning. Regards. Ginette.

Thomas wrote: 20 Jun

Thank you, Ginette: one more thing we share with you is you have an archangel protecting you and myself: I would never do anything detrimental not to make you a happy life even if it did not include me, way back when many years ago, we had a code of ethics in a motorcycle club I used to ride with.

Number one, I do not want to let you know what we did to child molesters: let me put it this way broken legs and broken ribs. It was a near-death experience for those people because child molesters never quit molesting children.

Number two, we never condoned raping women: there were consequences for that as well, not as severe as child molesters broken ribs for sure in a good beating, and then go back and beat them again.

And number three, never hit a woman, and the consequences were broken ribs and whatever what's done to that woman as far as the man hitting her, it was tenfold.

Now I'm not saying this to scare you, so please, maybe I should not be telling of this: it is not positive, but there are consequences for the actions, and that was the motto of our club. You will be held responsible for your actions.

Ginette, I want you to feel safe and comfortable with me and meet me because I will treat you like a queen. God bless with love and prayers, and I love you, Thomas.

Thomas wrote: 21 Jun

One other thing. I had to let you know, and I will think of it, but it slipped my mind, and my mind is usually like a trap. I keep thinking mainly about you, and I am also thinking about your mother and her well-being. Have a good day, sweetheart, and make sure to let your Mom know that someone other than yourself cares and loves for her. God bless.

Ginette wrote: 21 Jun

Hello Thomas,

Please forgive my delay when I do not message you on time and know that it is not intentional. Currently, I am so occupied with so much trying to do all possible for life to get balanced. It's not going as I want, but with God, nothing is impossible. I hope you're doing great, my heart goes to you as well each time, and you're also in my thoughts and prayers: that's what any right-minded person would like to leave a footprint on earth when they're gone.

Well, my Mom's fear isn't that you're a terrible person: she fears that I'm her only child, and her health is reduced, and anything happening to me negatively would mean heartbreak for her. I wish my Mom spoke excellent English to talk with you. I'll figure out on her having a word with you when I go to see her. Having an IQ is a gift not everyone has: no one was born without that person, only feel reluctant and most likely not use it. People say my IQ is very bright too, so having kids with you may make them very promising in mind and may achieve their goals quickly. Who knows.

I don't think our meeting was an accident. Let me tell you, I met a couple of guys from the dating site some your age, but we did not continue correspondence even for a week or two. And they started showing their true colors, like an older man who's a clergyman from Ontario. He was very indecent and very demanding. He started being too controlling, we met for the first time, and he wanted to love and pressure me.

I told my Mom about this, and she said he wasn't right for me. Mom said it's why he's alone. He hasn't been helpful to women in his life, and he's receiving his payback by being lonely. He may probably be lonely the rest of his life and may not have that care from anyone.

I had positive thinking about him, to live together and maybe the one in a few years to carter to him but he didn't think deeply. I stopped a couple of them, and I started focusing on you: I don't know what's a difference my Mom saw in you that she said to give you a try.

To be honest, I still get text messages from some guys, but I don't mind at all. Having self-pride is worth the precious or wealth of this cold world. We are not taking anything to our final resting place. Sad, but the truth.

I observed from you that you try to be impatient with me when you message me and don't get the answer. You already feel I have dumped you try to free your heart. I may be having positive thoughts about you while you're insecure: that's the comportment of a jealous man. If you are honest with me, you say many sad and negative things when you don't hear from me. Something serious would be going on, but you may be thinking I'm intentionally not responding.

Thomas, one thing you haven't understood about me is that I do not hope on others and never try to stick my nose in anyone's affairs: if it were the case, I would go on my knees to Sophie to stay with her knowing she's not considering my importance.

One of my main concerns is how you also go by daily: you're an adult and excuse me. It's not easy to live with such daily, and I do think much of your survival living all by yourself.

Apart from having a love for each other, I also care for you, and I want to make you feel special when we start to live together. It would be best if you didn't feel like you're to live a healthy life with me as the Thomas you have been before or what you're now.

Sure the best place for us to store our treasures is in heaven, our actual purpose is to seek the kingdom, and all will be given. I feel there's no real hope in this world. Earthly things are just to make life faster but are not there to qualify our walk with God, imagined most of the billionaires have gone to heaven already.

Thomas, my prayers are to have a man that respects me, cares, and can cry together and sing together with, isn't my prayers, but after I'm no more the young woman, I am what would be my achievement not being with a responsible person.

I only ask for a long life for you and me and the kids we will have: that's the most important thing first. I pray you're having a great night. Know that you're in my prayers, and I love you very much. Thanks for all your messages, and I look forward to hearing from you. Stay blessed! Kisses and hugs. Your girl from the north.

Thomas wrote: 22 Jun

My sweet Ginette, I'm happy to hear from you today, and I received your message on the telephone. My apologies for not being available. I was either in the kitchen was in the bathroom. I have been detrimental to you when I do not hear from you.

And you are more than likely right: I never thought of it before, maybe that's a sign of a jealous man that I never considered myself to be.

That's what I love about a woman's intuition: they can see things that a man cannot see.

Very kind, gentle intelligence with an intuition that was only sent from God into my life. And I quit questioning God and accept the fact that you are a beautiful young lady that cares about the character of my spiritual abilities and spiritual discernment.

I love God through Jesus Christ, our Lord's name, and the Holy Spirit, and I love you, for the beautiful young lady you are: there is only one of you and me, Ginette. And God loves us, and I am looking forward to our first face-to-face meeting whenever that happens.

And being offered a job on a commission to pass legislation and laws was what I prayed for the night before, not questioning that, and I thank you God through Jesus Christ, our Lord's, name for His will be done, not ours.

And I am happy for you, Ginette, to communicate with other gentlemen on the website. And I may have told you about the clergy of churches, my experience with the clergy is that they are not very good people in character. I find out they are people I do not want to associate with because I can feel the negative energy. If you read the chapter in my book, it's not a chapter I don't believe it is outlined, though called the soul's abomination. Very short, a couple of paragraphs, you might read and take a look.

I have not been alone for the last four years because I have not found any ladies: I have seen quite a few I cannot begin to count that would enjoy coming to live with me, for all the wrong reasons.

Until I. met you, I will have patience with no negativity, and I appreciate you bringing to mind my character defect. I can handle constructive criticism, and for that, I thank you. You are a precious soul.

And I pray to God never to hurt you in any way, shape, or form. I do not want you for your love or to make love with you immediately: that may or may not happen. Although I feel my heart, I will never meet a lady such as yourself.

And I will meet you again for eternity in heaven, and as I have mentioned before, I will always love you and do not think negatively of this thought, no matter who you're with or where you were. Only God knows that for sure: we do not.

Do you feel your mother would mind if I referred to her as a mom? And how would you feel if I referred to your mother as a mom? I heard one time that Canada's medical is free for all of its citizens. I listened to it a long time ago. I'm not sure if this is true today or not. Ginette, you are an angel and your mother, and as I have mentioned, you also are your mother's child. And she will be worried sick as any mother would, about her only precious child, and this is a fact, you will have to admit.

And if you feel it in your spirit that when we meet, your mother should be with you. I would most certainly understand that, and I think your mother would feel equally good about that. Your mother is probably worried sick about you quite often, more often than you think. May I ask you a question, and it is not harmful or anything to make you feel bad: this is not the intention.

I do not know how to put this, other than to ask you, why are you not close to your mother? I mean, as far as distance goes?

I realize that you talk to her quite often on the telephone and tell her everything, which makes her feel right. Until you hang up the phone, and then I would say she is, suddenly concerned, about your welfare and prays hard, that God will watch over you.

I have mentioned to you this before, that God has not only put a beautiful young angel into my life. But also that angel's mother, who is heaven-sent. I have to ask God because the miracles keep on coming: God, are you kidding me? And I get the answer through spiritual discernment in my spirit, that this is what I prayed for, and I better take great care with compassion, consideration, love, faith, understanding, all the positive things, and nothing negative.

So I thank you once again, Ginette, for pointing out my character defects. And you're right, as I look within my soul, I say to myself this beautiful young lady is proper when I said those negative things. When I had not heard from you in a while, it is because I was jealous. The last thing I ever thought I would be, and once again, I thank you for pointing out my character defects. I do not want to be that man, and I never want to be that man is spiritual discernment, from a precious beautiful soul.

And I thank you for the message you left today, and I went to a meeting tonight here in town at the grammar school. It is an opportunity to speak and help others: tonight's topic would include spirituality. Right up my alley, and I had to talk of a miracle.

And if you read the chapter in the book, called "God called me on the telephone," you will understand. I'm going to send you an episode in my next book, "soul sanctuary," it will be an attachment to this email. If you pleased to read it, I would appreciate it, and let me know what you think?

Ginette keeps in mind that if you are ever in a dangerous situation, yell loud "in Jesus Christ name, please help me," the evil will dissipate from you immediately. As you will read, " Lacey's story." Her name is Lacey: it happens in Elvira, New York.

Ginette, I love you for who you are: coming into my life has been an inspiration and a God-given gift, and for that, I love you so very much. I'm just going to say, God willing, and God's will be done, at the same time, I will acknowledge my love for him. I love you, Ginette, with xoxoxo.

Ginette wrote: 23 Jun

Good morning Thomas,

Finally, I can reply to all your messages, and I'll summarize all of your words in one word because I got many comments from you .

How have you been keeping since we last talk on the phone? I hope you're doing great. Do you think my Mom and I have an identical voice? I don't think so: I believe her view is a bit larger than mine. Her English isn't so good as mine, but she was happy hearing your voice for the first time. When we 3 are together, I'll be both of your translators.

I think the lady publisher isn't taking things for fun, lol, but I prefer a guy who shows and proves himself rather than throwing myself at him. There's a big difference between her character and that of mine. I wish her good luck. Let's also hope for the best about the possibility of having children with me: the best we can do is stay positive.

Thomas, to be honest, I'm fed up with this: I wasn't illegal then till now. It beats my imagination. I think what you can do is stop explaining about us, and you have done that enough already.

No, I didn't leave my job: I only went because of my Mom's health to at least be with her for a few days. I'll be traveling back to Montreal today. You're right. I'm no more at the address of Sophie's, I was staying in a motel, so it's where I'm going to be till I get a room.

Don't worry about how my Mom feels about you: she likes you and only wants the best for you and me, I. Thomas. I wish you know the kind of person I am when I say I love someone. It isn't a decision I make overnight, but something my heart accepts from deep in my heart.

So rest your mind and not allow your account to be insecure about me when someone's heart is mostly negative about others. It is impossible to see a reasonable person in your world: every person becomes an enemy.

You're just crucial as anyone else, and I do hold you in high regard. If others do not regard you, you know you have a family here in Canada that does. My prayers are with you as you wake up to go through your day. I'll try to give you a call before I leave Calgary. Warm hugs and kisses from the girl that loves you. Your sweetheart.

Ginette wrote: 23 Jun

Good morning Thomas,

It's always a pleasure hearing from you. I realize you wait eagerly for my messages, but you know I get so busy, and I feel bad not writing on time as you want. Good, you are trying to understand me: honestly, I wish I would get in touch right away. Please know my delay is never intentional okay?

How are you doing today? I hope you're starting your day very well. Mine is going great, and I'll see my Mom today and be back next week. I'll get in touch when I arrive. You're right. I tried to call, but you didn't pick. Don't worry about that, I understand.

I'm glad that you didn't feel I was criticizing you negatively, and I can tell you truly understand where I was coming from. As long we can understand one another, we will go along well, it's not wrong to disagree and agree that's our human nature, so I know when things do not seem to go right at times.

No relationship is successful without difficulties from the beginning, it is healthy, and I see we have had some such experience. You're right: the difference between women and men is that women tend to think deeply about what matters in a relationship and how well the link will succeed the little things that men can not see or notice. A lady is quickly embarrassed compared to a guy. You're a great person, Thomas, one that admits his flaws: not many guys will not want to be right.

I love you for this reason. I like your positive attitude towards your thorns: most people are shy about their limitations, but like you rightly said, it's your the torn in your flesh, so no need to regret it all the time. You're a lively guy and one that is full of humor. I appreciate that from you.

Well, I feel the same way about you first because you can see the difference between my character to that of those you have met and had some bad experience with. Not every person wants to hurt another: I experienced abuse from my high school boyfriend and always thought it was the same in every guy. Still, I see your character, and I can see how much you cherish me: I was a bit sad when you were so tough on me it reminded me of my past. So you know why I was not so gentle with you for some time.

I just hate to cry out loud: it's not my style. I don't like people knowing about my problems makes me feel like I'm pressuring others: one reason I was forced to leave Sophie's place because I do not want to be the reason she's stressed.

I know what I want. It wouldn't help you call my mother's

Mom better: you say, Diane, lol. Your question isn't wrong at all, and you see, I feel bad sometimes not living with my Mom, I left home not a long time ago. I visit my Mom regularly, depending on my schedule, and we frequently talk on the phone: she's not so bothered by that she knows I love her.

Enjoy. Ginette, your sweetheart.

Thomas wrote: 28 Jun

I love you and miss you, and I miss our emails together: I'm not sure if you cannot email me?

And your mother, I did not know if she cared for me or not, I am the right person, and I love to have fun and laugh and make other people laugh as well. It kind of takes their mind off of their trials and tribulations: that's one of my spiritual gifts. To make people happy and laugh.

I'm not sure how you feel about me, or if you change your mind about us, I'm excited to get started on our life. If you do not think that will happen for one reason or another, please let me know because I am anxious to get started. It is a romance novel, and ladies will just love reading if you're not interested or do not want to write anymore.

It kind of hurts my heart Ginette that you're not happy, or you did not sound satisfied yesterday from what I could feel. I could be wrong, and it may have been just because your mother was right there, and I can understand that. You do know I love you very much, and I always will.

I care about you, and God loves you, and God loves you, and you have a good day, sweetheart. I pray that you can give me a telephone call. I should be home at about 1 PM, after that you can call me. I get excited about hearing your voice. This time I will not laugh like an idiot because I'm so excited: I will try to tone it down like a moron, smile. If there's anything I can do for you or your mother, please do not hesitate to let me know, okay?

You have a good day, sweetheart, and I love you with hugs and kisses. I would not want to hurt you in any way or break your heart. I want to make you happy, and I would certainly enjoy our meeting at your convenience at one point in time. I love you, and I triple adore you. Love you, and make sure and let your mother know my prayers are with her.

Thomas wrote: 29 Jun

Sweetheart sends me a one-liner letting me know that you made it back okay. I'm not going to say, home, this is our home where we live.

God only knows why you are going back to Montréal because I have no clue. Oh yes, and you know, but I'm a little perplexed as to why you are drawn to go to Montréal? It's not because of your friends: otherwise, you would not be staying in a motel. I can only think of the only reason, and I am only applying this to myself, you will understand.

When I beat up two cops and was sent to Arizona state mental institution for six months, I was on probation for six months after getting out. I could not leave the county that I lived in.

Another time, I received a ticket for driving 3 miles an hour in the fast lane on a Friday night, during rush hour traffic. And the Arizona Highway Patrol had to do what they call the round- robin, going back and forth behind me just to slow down the traffic. When they finally pulled me over, they asked me if there was anything wrong with my car? I realized that I had over 1 mile of traffic backed up behind me.? I wish I could have said the word "yes." I could not even talk, and I was on drugs and alcohol. I had to do eight weeks in work furlough for felony vehicular driving. That felony is still on my records, and I could not leave the county once again.

Those are the reasons I could not reject without checking with my parole officer first and getting permission. And you mentioned to me at one point in time and you would not be able to come until December. I believe that's what you said. I was just curious if any of my situations applied to you?

You can tell me the truth, Ginette, and I will understand that the truth will always set you free no matter what the situation. And I would love you even more, and excuse me for mentioning this. I said I was going to keep this positive and my imagination as always. No matter what you have done, what you are doing now, or what you plan on doing, you just keep in mind that I will always love you because you are my girl.

I would have an accurate understanding of the reason why you are drawn to Alberta, Canada.

I'm not sure what your intentions are? I only wish to make you happy, loving kisses, your chatting friend, a telephone friend, a teacher, a potential boyfriend. Your future husband, with whom you would like to have children? I love you.

Thomas wrote: 29 Jun

I just thought I would check-in and say good night and that I love you very much: of course, you know me better than that. I was to say than that, Mr. motormouth, smile. Did you not tell me about your mode of travel? And I read where you mentioned you would be getting on a train?

If you can believe this or not, the only train I have ever been on was a freight train. When we were kids, we would hitchhike over the mountain to see a movie on Friday nights.

And sometimes a freight train would be going by really slow, and we would all jump on. And then we would jump off, maybe 1/2 mile down the tracks, just for something to do. And that is the only train I have ever been on, that I can remember. So when we get together, you must take me on a train ride, that would be cool, I think. Do you get to see the countryside? And do they have sleepers where you could spend the night?

Do you know what I feel from your spirit? Is that your past was not that good, and you may be ashamed of some things you did, as we all are. But we cannot dial back the clock for one second. We had to go through those lessons to learn them. I feel that you are a beautiful young lady that found the Lord and wants to change her life from her past life.

I could be wrong, and I usually am. No matter what I say, I am not trying to discredit you or make you feel bad about yourself, or dredge up some memories. No matter what I mean, I will always love you: let me say that again, no matter what I write, I will always love you.

Thomas wrote: 29 Jun

How are you today, sweetheart? I pray things are going well, I miss you, which we were together, and I pray for us both.

Because my love for you is far more important to us and God's will for us than to do anything negative that would jeopardize our love for one another.

I was tired yesterday and last night, and I tried to make it a point to at least once usually. Tell you that I love you, and my prayers are with you, and do not forget to say your prayers. I am happy that your mother was delighted to hear my voice: I care what you think and smile.

As far as your mother's voice and your voice, there is a significant similarity. You would not know the difference because you know your mother and your mother knows you. Someone who has not heard your mother and has heard you would note there is a definite similarity.

Anyway, I love you, and I will keep communications positive: that's the way our life is going to be together, positive and happy through the grace of God. I know, I do not know too much about your past, nor do I care to learn of the details of being a human. When you get the opportunity to read the book "Soul Journey," finally, you will know me better. And you will know my past, and it was not all good. Do I have any regrets? No regrets, are not forgiving yourself, and the best resentment for regrets is forgiveness of self. The best revenge for grievances is forgiveness.

I am finally glad to hear from you and your plans for going back to Montréal: evidently, that is where you feel comfortable, and that where you have friends. I'm not sure what your intentions are as far as you and me? I pray that it is for the best for both of us, whatever your plans are. If you want to make God laughs, plan your life. A smile I do care about you. I will always love you with compassion and trust with love and faith from God, and that you could take to the bank.

If you would like to get together and come and see me, that will be your decision. I am not going to make you feel obligated or like you feel obligated. I want to make you happy in your life. Whatever you decide between you and me over the emails, we can do it. I think you remember all the questions I had asked you at one point in time? I pray to God you do not feel offended or that I hurt you in any way by asking those personal questions? I have a good feeling God has let me know this through the

Holy Spirit. So if you care to write this email, sweetheart, I will have to ask you many personal questions. I think the questions I will be asking you will understand why because the answers will have to go into the book.

Anyway, have a good day, honey, and if you call, I will be happy to hear your voice. And when you talk to your mother again, you always make sure and tell her that my prayers are with her and that I give her my best wishes. I love you with hugs and kisses.

Thomas wrote: 30 Jun

The question is, where is my tiny little pumpkin breath?

It takes a beautiful young lady such as yourself to keep this boy honest, and this boy is reasonable to the woman he loves for eternity. Ladies that attempt to email me, I simply say, "I am engaged to be married to a beautiful young lady named Ginette from Canada."

And that is the last I hear from them, even ladies I have known for quite some time, thank God for my beautiful wife. After four years, finally, it feels free not to be bugged by the buggies, and I like that. It gives me more time to spend with my sweetheart. If you get the opportunity, honey, only if the spirit moves you, please give me a call. If you care to provide me with your phone number, I can call you at a specific time designated? I'm not sure about you, but Satan is biting at my heels like I knew he would.

God has brought to me that I feel a sincere obligation to care in the form of an angel. I want this beautiful angel to know that she can trust her man that God has put into her life. Well, sweetheart, I will wait either to get a call from you or an email. I always get excited when I see an email from you and double surprise when I pick up the phone, not knowing it's you: that is the real surprise. Make sure and let your mother know that my prayers are with her.

What have you told your mother about the two of us? Does she know that we are in love? You are so fortunate to be the only child, and sometimes families are okay. And sometimes they are not, and there's always the greedy bunch in every family.

Sweetheart, I just love you so much, I miss you, and I would care to be with you. God willing, it will happen when God wants it to happen. I just get anxious just wanting to see you for the first time, is going to put a smile on my face from ear to ear, and I'm not going to stop smiling. I love you, honey, hugs, and kisses.

JULY 2018, ROMANTIC MEMOIRS FROM HEAVEN

Ginette wrote: 1 Jul 2018,

Good morning Thomas,

I wasn't intentionally keeping silent from your messages. It was a long way from Calgary to Montreal, with no direct trains. So I needed to stop in Toronto and board the plane to Montreal since it was expensive to fly direct. Thank the good Lord that I got here safely. How have you been keeping? I realize you have been impatient not to hear from me and have started thinking about so much once again.

Ginette wrote: 4 Jul

Happy Independence Day! I hope you're having a good day so far. Sorry for my delay. I have been busy since I got back here: okay, I can message now.

Well, I'm a determined person, but it does not mean I take life too seriously. I'm a lively person, but when one has too much on one plate, life does not seem to be that joyful: that's what is happening currently.

I'm glad that you try to understand me: I feel you don't trust me or think negatively about me because you have listened to too many people about us. I also have people to listen to, but I prefer to handle my life and let God do the rest. Still, you weren't doing the same, and you instead take me in front of others to tell you how they feel about me.

I have forgiven you, and I honestly don't hold things against people. Like I said before, if you don't hear from me, it does not mean it's over between us because I'm busy: we have different lives, Thomas. You're mostly at home on your computer, and I'm not mostly home or on a computer as I have to go to work.

However, I appreciate your time in messaging me, but you know, with all the messages you send, I must read everything and take my time to express my thoughts in my notes. I do enjoy your words, but you know there is so much to learn from you.

Yes, you're right: we are at the same pace, and I think we get along: if not, we couldn't have been in touch till now. When two spirits are connected, it's not possible to disconnect: that's what I think exists between us.

I agree a man will always be a man, and same with a lady, we think differently, but that doesn't mean we can't understand and get along. We disagree about things, but it's intelligent people that overcome quickly and moves forward. I seem like a girl that isn't that responsible looking, but I do, and it's within my heart. People who don't know me or interact with me think most of the time difference, but I'm just me. I'm glad you say I'm teaching you many things: you're doing the same as well.

I learn a lot from you. Yes, I realize you hurt me most of the time, and I almost want to quit, but I know you don't mean harm. It's only your harsh jokes, but with your background as a former soldier, it is understandable that your lifestyle is a rough one, lol. People learn about one another. It's a whole life process, so I can be patient and not take things too seriously with you. I know you're the right person Thomas.

Depression is a killer: too many people struggle with it, and I don't want that from you or me: we do not need to be depressed. Alcohol and drugs are so evil: it has ruined the lives and happiness of many people. I know about myself that I always stay real with people I want to be me.

I'm never afraid to say my heart to anyone, no matter the person's age or status. I'm a respectful person but only speak the truth of what's going on in my heart. I respect you a lot

Thomas and love you, but I must be real when I feel things aren't going right. I'm glad we both understand. Thanks for all the pictures: they're beautiful and are a complete history of you. You came from afar till now, and I can see God has been with you. It would be great when you fly here, but depending on how convenient these are things to figure out, we will see. Writing our book isn't something that would be done in a hurry. Let's continue to pray about the best way all will go according to God's plan.

Enjoy the rest of your day until I hear from you again. Love kisses and hugs. Your love.

Ginette wrote: 12 Jul

Why we wear them

The sleeve, I couldn't have been honest enough to give you my real name, phone, and address. I think I have proven myself beyond all doubts. If you want to exchange my presence with you to help, it's like paying for sex from me like a person involved in prostitution. From the beginning about my past, Thomas, I have told you it was horrid, and that shouldn't judge me, the fact that my history was terrible and realize and have accepted Christ.

It shouldn't be any person's responsibility to qualify my life as positive or negative: lets God allow me, with all my lousy past, to be my judge! You have your bad history, and you have no regrets, and I'm glad you understand that my problem is not you really, but those you keep sharing me with, Thomas, there are worse people more than me that have realized and become better people. My only crime was being a model, and the life of a model is very much not a perfect one, but I needed to survive.

I'll be honest with you, yes, I told you December would've been the best time to travel out of the country and not because I'm on probation: why? If you'll be honest, I didn't have in mind to meet someone called Thomas, and I only registered on the dating site to meet a man. That we can know each other and in term meet, that was how I thought, I didn't purposely register to attend a specific person but one that would be a kind, respectful, loving, and caring person. I think that's what every decent girl would wish. I'm not a good writer, but since God made it possible for you and me to meet, I thought it was good to appreciate and accept what you like doing.

Then we do it together, but the way you start to take things makes me feel pressured even though I love you and want to get involved. In writing with your help to have a happy life together but not necessarily mean that I'll just abandon my life in another country and just get on the plane because the guy I met wants that. Understand you're in touch with another human being in another country and has a life: one must plan for things before making a decisive move. Are you not because I may be younger, but I'm knowledgeable, and I do go by my feelings?

I'm in a motel room not because I have no friends here, but they are jealous of me, and they think I'm going mad over an older man! I wouldn't stay with a friend that I must be in pretense and hiding to speak with you, friends who want me to go out with guys of their choice, not mine. Do you understand? I have seen too many things about living in a brief period of my life, and my understanding is just not the same as Sophie and Sandrin.

They are only interested in plays with their experience with young guys who are only heard-brokers. They'll realize I'm not stupid for not following them later. So please, let's take things slowly: a lot is going on in my life. If you feel I'm not the one for you because of being honest with you, you're free to check around for a girl of my character and qualities. I'm not in Montréal for any other reason, but it's because I work here: I wouldn't overlook my job because you give me the impression that life will be better. I can already see how much you were struggling to help imagine being with you, you'll dictate to my life, and I may end up regretting and having my friends that are already mocking me laugh in my face. There are many things I'm considering.

You know there's not much I can contribute to your family matters as a stranger to all this. I realize material wealth is an immense tragedy in many families. Humans only need a little to survive, but because people have too many things in their hearts makes them greedy and, in terms, makes others lose their lives. Your brother dies because of pressure and also drugs: the drug is a big problem for too many people.

Thomas, I'll only give up on you for one reason, your lack of trust and people getting involved in our affairs. Not many people that wish you or me very well. They may be friends or family, but life's happiness is individually, after all.

Of course, my Mom knows about us: she knows you are friends with me for a relationship: that's why she told me to be careful before my heart is broken again. Can you do one thing? Stop measuring me or our relationship with people. When I come to live with you, you will not need to say anything people will see for themselves: for now, they'll only say negative things about me to discourage me.

I have the same experience here as well when I measured you or our relationship, and there are waves of laughter they say negative things my only best person in all this is Diane, my Mom thank God she's still alive if not my heart would be broken each time.

Thanks for all the romantic things been said. I appreciate your love for me. I hope you're having a good day, and I look to hearing from you again. All my love to you. My regards to you.

Your love ♡ .

I had no parental support like other privileged girls after I lost my dad .

Staying in Montreal isn't about following my heart but the opportunity to work here and support my life and mother. I got friends in Calgary, the same as here, and I understand why you find it challenging whenever you hear about Montréal: you think about two things, maybe I got a boyfriend here. I'm not going to make it to Arizona, so you feel uneasy understanding my honesty. Think about this. Another thing is, you're in so much hurry because of love or to write books with you?

I don't know anyone on fraud watch, I haven't been to Russia before, but I have registered on a couple of dating sites: some may have been foreign sites. Well, I don't know, but I have not met exciting guys. I registered in some places, but some times I don't even recheck them.

Thomas wrote: 22 Jul

When no one else can understand me when everything I do is wrong, you give me hope and consolation, and you give me the strength to carry on. And you're always there to lend a hand, and everything I do that's the wonder, the wonder of you. And when you smile, the world is brighter, you touch my hand, and I am a king. Your kiss to me is worth a fortune: your love for me is everything. I guess I'll never know the reason why you love as you do and because that's the wonder of you. I love you, sweet Ginette: you're the precious light that shines forth from the beacon of my heart. That will never separate us or bring us apart. God bless with love and prayers. Hugs and kisses, I love you.

3RD BATTALION FOR THE MARINES

6th Marine Regiment

2nd Marine Division

Camp Lejeune, NC The Ready Battalion-Never To Quito

During World War I, the French Government awarded decorations for exceptionally meritorious conduct in action to 156 American units varying in the team twice decorated with the Croix de Guerre with Palms, was entitled to a braided and knotted cord and known as the French Portégé, in the green and red colors of the Croix de Guerre. The French Portégé becomes part of the unit's uniform, so cited authorizing all organization members. To wear the decoration on the left shoulder of the dress Uniform, as long as they remain members of the organization.

According to Larousse's Grand Dictionary of the XIX Century, the French Portégé originated by Alva's Duke. After a unit of Flemish troops, a Spanish general had made a rather hasty withdrawal from the battlefield. The Duke ordered: "that any further misconduct, on the part of these troops, should be punished by hanging, without regard for rank or grade. The Flemish warriors, determined to re-establish themselves in the good graces of their commander, wore--as a reminder of their disgrace--coiled around one shoulder. A rope in the shape of a hangman's noose dangled a long spike at the end of which. In their next battle, the Flemish troops fought so gallantly that the loop and spike became a mark of distinction and honor.

The French Portégé is a decoration instituted by Napoleon for units that distinguished themselves in battle. It was revived during World War I and was awarded by the French Ministry of War to organizations cited more than once in the French Army. Third--Croix de Guerre with palm (Green/Red). The Marine Corps and the French Portégé.

In 1918, Marines of the Sixth Regiments, by their heroic deeds of valor, inscribed the names of influential and brilliant battles on the pages of Marine Corps history, as well as on their regimental battle colors.

They have the singular honor of being the only regiment in the American Expeditionary Force to receive three citations. Two in the Orders of the Army and one in the Orders of the Corps.

The French Portégé and the Croix de Guerre with two Palms and one gold Star.

As a Second Battalion member, Sixth Marines, we are authorized to wear the French Portégé as a part of our uniform. Marines originally earned this award as an individual decoration through their heroism, bloodshed, and ultimate sacrifice in Belleau Wood, Soissons, and Champagne's fields. Since World

War I, Marines of 2d Battalion, 6ᵗʰ Marines have worn the French Portégé. As a unit decoration carrying it into battle at Guadalcanal, Tarawa, Okinawa, and many other campaigns, listed in this website's article, "Battalion History."

This braided rope and spike embodies and recalls Marines' gallant conduct and fighting spirit who have gone before us. It marks us as warriors, an independent battalion, and a grand regiment. Wear the French Portégé with pride, dignity, and honor and always remember in whose footsteps we tread.

Above: A Marine Sgt. wearing the French Portégé on his Service Dress "Alpha" uniform. The Service Dress uniform used to be the first uniform worn in the field during this period. The

French Portégé on the Service Dress "Alpha" uniform.

AUG 2018, ROMANTIC MEMOIRS FROM HEAVEN

Who makes you happy?
Somebody who doesn't complicate your life.

Ginette wrote: Aug 3

Hi honey,

I waited for your message last night and today but not sure you made it home yet, and I hope you're doing good and everything is going well. It's a bit late here now, so I'll get some sleep shortly. Have a great night.

Thomas wrote: Aug 4

Thank you Ginette, I'm fine, I've just been listening to the Bible all day and reading Scripture. In the middle of some family issues, trials, and tribulations, we all go through. We are not alone, and we are still blessed: it could always be worse.

Have you ever thought of maybe God wanted you to change your directions in life? And possibly Grab a suitcase and flight to Arizona,? It would be beneficial for both of us, and God willing this is what I will pray. I'm not sure I understand what you're going through in your life through the grace of God, and in Jesus Christ, the Lord's name, I pray that everything works out for you.

My heart and my love will always be with you no matter where you are or whatever you decide to do. And I can only be here for you through these letters of a love that I have for you, and the feelings that I would like to show you in the spiritual togetherness that would be God's will with respect, kindness, and compassion.

You'll never know the way that I love you until we are together. We are the lucky ones to be inspired by faith from God above. I have sent love spiritually, and we are the blessed ones, put your hand in mine. Baby you don't know what it's like to love somebody, there's a light, a certain kind of light that draws us together, and it will not stop shining because I love somebody. I pray you to know what it's like, I need somebody to love.

Somebody said you have a new friend, and there's a big black sky over my home, here I sit dancing alone. I'm spinning around, and I'm right here, why can't you come to me. I'm not the guy you're taking home, and I keep dancing on my own.

Praying to God and continuously alone, I'm not the guy you're taking home, but I sit here and think of you. I'm all alone, you're far away, but still, so near, can he love you better than I can?

I'm imagining him kissing you, and that's okay. And that I'm sitting here not entirely alone, you are my guardian angel in my spirit, for eternity. We have a love that was sent from heaven and God above, and I will always to be here if you need me, I love you, we will be together one day, just not yet.

Thomas wrote: 7 August

Thomas would like to prove his friendship to Ginette. Two friends, Thomas and Ginette thought they would like to take a walk in the woods together to enjoy one another's company and companionship as well as pleasant conversation, looking at nature in its natural habitat. The wildlife and to enjoy the atmosphere breathing fresh air. Thomas had the backpack and had a few items in the pack, and of course, lunch. Thomas and Ginette were going to sit down and eat together after hiking a distance.

When all of a sudden out of nowhere Thomas and Ginette came upon a bear, Thomas immediately drops down on the ground, pulled his tennis shoes out of the backpack, and was taking his hiking boots off. Ginette said to Thomas, "you cannot outrun that bear," and Thomas said, "I do not have to outrun that bear: "all I have to do is outrun you."

The moral of the story, John: 15,13, There is no greater love than this that Ginette lay down her life for her excellent friend Thomas. smile, the devil made me do it, LOL.

Ginette wrote: 9 August

Sorry I was so tired last night and went to bed early. I'm glad to see your messages. It's always a pleasure to hear from you. I didn't call you yesterday I'll soon. Ah, a sale lady sounded like me lol funny. A great cook seems excellent, and I'll see if you are when I come over, I'll be your judge in the kitchen! I know how you feel concerning what I'm facing right now, I'm more hurt than as I'm the one in the actual situation. I understand your suggestion, my love, and honestly, I love to come to you, but like I have told you before, not until December God willing.

Typically December is vacation time, and it is a convenient time for many people to travel. This is something I have prayed about, but you try to insist, it makes me feel you want my presence there at any cost. Not even thinking I have a life here, and there are many preparations for traveling to another country, not a nearby city. I wish you knew how much I want to be with you, but it seems like you don't think it's going to happen.

My mind is made up of living with you all my life, but you are not trying to understand me too. Honey, I'm not a lazy person at all: I would never want to sit idle while you alone provide when we start to live together. I know we have a lot of work to do with the books and our kids so imagine how much I'm planning on moving it seems natural to you, but moving isn't that easy, so please give me some time.

Good to keep the commandments, but know the commandments are not there to secure our going to heaven. The only way is through one means, and that way is the gospel of Jesus Christ that brings us total salvation and eternal security. That as long we receive Christ with all our hearts that He's the only Son of God, the truth and the light and that only through Him we can make heaven. The commandments are to cause us to see who we are, like seeing ourselves in the mirror-like you rightly put it. I'm not unrighteous, and I may seem from a physical viewpoint but in God's sight.

I was just a bit sad the way you put things at times, what do you mean by if I do good things will follow, and bad things bad will follow? I don't think even when we master the commandments can make us perfect in God's sight. Because He said we humans are like filth in His sight, our only real hope is salvation in Christ. Because we can't be holy in our flesh, and we are not to judge others.

I have read the paragraph where you talked about the commandments and the rest. Honestly, they're good topics, and a Christian can not live without those, they're there to help us guide us in our earthly walk, to live with each other with no trouble.

I'm glad that you did share these with me, but the way you put them didn't go down well, make me feel less holy. Please don't get me wrong I truly appreciate your love and teachings. But you know there were things you misunderstood about me.

Thanks for having the trust and confidence in me to share what is going on with you as well. I'll get ready now to get a shower and leave. Let me know if I said anything wrong, and I'm not too important to say sorry.

I have forgiven you and will forever love you also. As long as we two can disagree and agree, then we will face the storm together and win together. Love you so much, my endless love.

Enjoy the rest of your day. Your wife.

Ginette wrote: 10 August

Sorry for my delay in reply: it is never intentional, okay. I feel I must take my time to always correspond to the man I love, especially when I have to take my time to respond to every bit of your message. How was your night, sweet man? I hope you slept well and dream of us. I always do! Well, I think parting the Red Sea would be the job of you since Moses was a male lol the women-only passed through after He did the miracle! Lol

Well, if you keep shooting your legs, you wouldn't have toes left to climb, so will you keep shooting in your legs? Which one do you choose? I love the way you're a sweetheart. You're such a fun person. Do you want to pinch me on my cheek?

I know it's my buttocks you are thinking about, lol! I'll always help you keep you on track, my love, we belong to each other.

Those that are in love would ever want the best for each other. I'm a lively person and not the earnest person you think I like laughter too and fun for the most part, I wouldn't hide my feelings from you and will always say it as it is.

True, not we may seem closer, but it does not mean I can travel if not ready yet. I'll it's no big deal about it just need to straighten up a few things here before. I didn't mean that it should necessarily be in December that people travel, I was trying to tell you it would be convenient for me during that. I'm not trying to be everybody or go with the flow I have choices. I hope you understand.

Well, I agree we need a law for an orderly living, thanks for going on details, know I do learn a lot from you whenever you write to me. It's always great, and I appreciate that. Just asking, do you care? I'll end here for now.

I look forward to hearing from you — your Love ♡ .

Ginette wrote: 11 August

Good morning Thomas my love,

It's always great hearing from you: you make me feel good.

How did your night go? I hope it was good. Mine was excellent, and I was so tired last, so I didn't reply till now.

I didn't ask negatively at all, just to see what you meant. I know we are bound to love each other till the end, and our relationship would be a blessing to others to bring smiles to their faces. In bringing a smile to another person's face, you must be smiling yourself, that's sure you're a happy person who wants to make another person happy. I hope to understand. Well, I thought to respond to you since I did hear from you after you said you were going to message back. I know you were busy. Oh yes, I always let my mom know you said hi. I called the other day, and she was happy that you think about her. You have a great day morning sweetheart. My heart goes out to you and all my love . Your love.

Ginette wrote: 13 August

Good morning my love,

Sorry, it has taken me a few days to get back to you. Things are a bit busy the past few days, but I'm glad I can message you now. How have you been? I hope that you have been keeping well. By God's help, I'm also doing great. It's always a pleasure to get back to you and hear from you about how life is treating you as well.

Thanks for being understanding, I appreciate that rest assure that you're the one I think about and genuinely want to be with you. It's not so long, and we will finally be together. Well, people say I speak good English, but I feel I still need to get better and better lol. What things did I mention that makes you laugh? Are you trying to tease me, right? 😄

The story of Paul formerly Saul in the Bible is so exciting, and he was a thorn in the flesh of Christians at first. And then the Romans became torn in his flesh for the very gospel He hated that's a significant occurrence in the Bible.

You're so right, lay down one's own life for your neighbor is something that is beyond human imagination. It's only when you have faith and love of Jesus Christ that such can occur. Only those in Christ can comprehend. The Bible is a book that touches all aspects of our lives.

Sure instant karma does exist, and I have seen that too, you're another testimony of that. I like where you talked about your Dad's friend calling you one day after you prayed to be sober, that's the power of God beyond human control. He is the one that allows no matter what, whether positively or negatively, for his glory.

Thanks for asking, I'm doing great and hope you're too, it's only the issue with getting a room that I'm still looking forward. I can imagine all that needs to be done with your family issues, but nothing is impossible, only prayers we need, and the rest will get in place. You'll continue to be in my prayers. Honey thinks mostly about the future and is positive, and no one knows their time on earth.

Let's continue to want for the best okay. I know, and I can see from the pictures you sent me then, I truly understood you were a hard-working person when you were much better. The past is the past: we focus on the future. As we live together, we will write more books, and our writing will inspire many souls to see the reason to give their lives to God.

Even if you're gone before me, I'll always continue your work that wherever you're, you'll always smile for that reason. Our meeting is never a mistake but a miracle, sure I have had miracles happen in my life, where God took me from till today, when I look back, I just praise God. Our kids will be glad to have such parents:

With faith, I know we will be the happiest people in the world.

Anyway, my love, I'll go for now. I am looking forward to hearing from you. I'll get get back to work now. I love you so much. Hugs and kisses .

Thomas Wrote: 14 August

For security and God with unshakable faith, I can believe do that through my writing. I miss physical work because I used to be a hard worker, like seven days a week, 12 to 16 hours a day. I believe God was preparing me for writing to share the miracles that we have experienced throughout our lives. I know you have plenty of miracles that have happened in your life up until the time we have met. God willing, I pray to provide you with a safe environment for not only our children but for yourself as well.

I will write more I feel a need to send this to you right now what I was going to say I forgot where my last email. I left off, God is not finished with either of us, and I cannot see a God-loving God put us together. And calling me home anytime soon, I'm still behind the eight ball with God and have a lot more ground to make up. From all the evil stuff I did when I was using and drinking all those years, and God knows, that spiritually.

I love you to pieces to pieces I will send you another email to pick up where I'm leaving off. I just want you to feel comfortable and safe in our environment together. I love you, my sweet Ginette. God blessed with love and prayers, and let us not forget to say our prayers. Remain God- conscious through Jesus Christ, our Lord's name, and let the Holy Spirit work through us to help others.

Thomas wrote: 15 August

First and foremost, you are one of my guardian angels and my spiritual guide to keeping me on track. I will not be where I am right now if we're not for you. That we were meant to be together forever and eternity, and that will make them happy.

I have been to Malta where your father was born, and the apostle Paul was shipwrecked. I was proud to wear the French Portégé, United States Marine Corps, for fighting the battle of Bella Woods in France during World War I.

Age does not make a difference because the two of us, will see the second coming of the Lord Jesus Christ at some point in time in our lives: we are equally yoked spiritually.

God willing, we are going to have children together: we will live out our lives together in happiness joyous and free, making each other laugh continuously. Helping other souls get to heaven, through our writing and just meeting other people, we are supposed to meet. I cannot help but think that your father put us together spiritually, along with Apostle Paul and Jesus Christ, our Lord.

The downside, we are going to be attacked spiritually by evil forces, and we will know them when we see them or get near them. Together we will fight this battle and have fun through Jesus Christ, our Lord.

As time goes by, more similarities will come to us, or we may recognize when they do. We have a love for one another that neither of us has ever experienced before. And that will be a miracle that could only happen through the Holy Spirit and God, our Father in heaven, and Jesus Christ, our Lord.

John 3:16. For God so loved the world that he gave His only begotten Son that whoever shall believe in Him shall not perish and have everlasting life.

postscript: My goal until we see one another this I pray, and say your prayers they are powerful, I care and I love you. I pray for you, Ginette, that everything is going well in your life because you are my wife for the rest of our experience. We will be in heaven together for eternity with our children. God willing xoxox.

Ginette wrote: 16 August

Good afternoon my love Thomas,

I guess you wonder why it takes some time to reply, it is never intentional, but I feel I must take my time to respond to all you have written. How is my handsome man doing? I hope you're having a blessed day. Mine is going great and busy but thought to reply as possible as I can. You're always in my heart and prayers, my love.

I like your writing about us and your sense of humor, you're a fun person, and that's the kind of person I would like around me.

You are not taking things too seriously because life in itself has so much already.

I think we are the right match, and that lady psychologist in your story of you was right: every young girl would want those qualities. But does necessarily if a person can accept another and their character defects, this way, you have forgotten to follow your thought but that of God. You must be a mind reader lol. It's just me!

And I like how God has dealt with me to accept you as my lover — not looking for things from my viewpoint. I feel so connected to you physically and spiritually, and I can feel the Holy Spirit moving in the lives of both of us. The same way you think about me, your mind being flooded with me it's the same for me as well. Well, looking at your age, and mine seems like our destiny is short, but believe me, no one knows God's plan and timing. So we rest our hearts and look forward to what God wants to do in our lives He knows more than us.

We have a lot of work to do when starting to live together.

Writing and making an impact on the lives of many people. Well, they say that there's time for everything: God knows the reason you never known love for this long. I believe it's because He was preparing you for me to show the love that you have never shown before. We were in 2018, so imagine how long He has been developing this moment!

To realize I don't have the passion for writing until I met you. I'm enjoying that now lol.

Yes, I do agree on that connection about my country Malta and that of apostle Paul, my dad, you and I: it's something that makes me think deeply.

You see, my background is from there, you have been there and then apostle Paul has a great history there, who knew you were going to come across this connection in your life? If it's not God that has planned all this till now! Wow, God is alive!

Well for me I have no idea why I love so much, I think I'm just doing God's will. I'll always understand you and put you on track no matter what. I have decided in my heart that you're truly the love of my life, being your guardian angel makes me very happy, and I'm glad you can see that.

Thanks very much for thinking about me: it makes me feel you genuinely care. I know you do, and believe me, I have never doubted your love for me the same way I never doubt my love for you. We are the only ones that truly understand what we feel for one another.

I'll be patient though it's not easy waiting, God is the patience it's His second name, so I'll exercise patience.

Hmmm, I have forgiven you and will always forgive you because I know you're a silly guy wouldn't get angry like before lol .

Am I with a child? Well, I think so! I would be the happiest woman alive to be carrying a child for! Mrs. Ginette would be great!

Well, I do read every message you send, the reason I don't write back right away is that I know you'll message more. So I wait until I know you're looking up to hearing from me before I can. Good idea, right?

Honey, I know it's a pleasure of writing, but also be sure that no publisher is going to take advantage of the fact you love writing. And demand you to giving funds, understand that you're no more alone, you have a child of someone in your life.

You can not find a publisher more than the love of your life. You remember the publishers from Florida and Germany I was the one that did put you on track.

So know I'm not trying to be controlling but to be sure you're doing the right thing. We have a future together, so I must be there to discuss things. I hope you don't find this like I want to control you. I want to be there for you. Love you so much, my love. Take care, and enjoy the rest of your day. You are thinking about you. 🐵 And kisses .

Ginette wrote: 17 August

Sure we will be the best partner, and we get along so well already, so I don't think we have many worries. My simple answer to your question concerning why you love me so much is we were connected before we were born! You were busy finding the wrong ribs. That's why you were never happy in the past relationships, and I think I was the crazy rib bone of my high school boyfriend: that's why we were never compatible. We are the right match: that's why you can't get your mouth or minds out of me and the same with me too.

Well, it is difficult not to respond to any of your messages.

They all are essential to me: reading them is like I'm right there with you! Well, I think the best thing you could do is those books you have written. You can do checks on them in case no errors, and you can then add and subtract to make the books extravagant.

This way, you wouldn't need much editing from the publisher. It would save you funds and time.

After you're sure that all you have written are in order, then you can take it one at a time: this way, our audience will keep looking instead of being boring if you write one at a time you have more room to please your audience. I'm not much of a writer like you, but my simple ideas can change many things, those that can benefit you. The publisher wouldn't tell you to stop writing as long they're getting paid, I think the reason for writing is to have an audience base.

Just one book can make you known, then thinking more would do that. One way that can have us with a broad audience is the internet, and just the social network can change a lot of things. Have people willing to hear from you more, I think sites like Facebook, Twitter, and Amazon would make our writing known faster. My idea is okay.

You're so right honey, your definition of a Christian is on point if you ask many people they would only tell you that a Christian is a follower of Christ, that is just limited to me. I think as you rightly put it makes a lot of sense. Being an all-new person in the spirit and not seeing things from the earthly point of view.

Well, no matter your past must be like as long we love each other, I'm glad and would never judge you based on your history, the way you don't judge me base on my past as well. As long we have this in mind, there would be any reason not to love each day.

I read the letter you sent to the church, and there are wicked people in this world. God will always protect you, and I'll keep putting issues with your family before God.

There's nothing too hard for Him.

I wanted to tell you to keep my Mom in prayers, and she's supposed to be traveling to Europe to meet with my Dad's extended family, not sure we had similar issues concerning family. Still, there are no fights: they want to show my Mom some essential things for the family there. She will be traveling with them, so I need your prayers. I'm praying that things go successful so that I'm December I will be able to travel to you.

Once what my Mom is going to settle get in place, there will be much for her to live on, and I wouldn't have to worry too much. So keep us in prayers. I'll let you know how things go.

I'll get ready to leave for work now. Thanks so much for all your kind messages. Enjoy your day, my love. Kisses and hugs .

Thomas wrote: 17 August

For keeping me on track once again, you already have a child, me, smile. Thank you so much for that very long email I always look forward to receiving one from you. And I also realize I know you are a very busy lady because you are my girl.

It floods back memories that I may not have forgotten, and I feel it is good to feel those feelings. From time to time, not forget those precious moments in time. Like I had mentioned, thank you, my guardian angel, for keeping me on track,

It may not be a bad idea if I also had your current telephone number, not that I am going to call you without you first give me the okay. I have to know is much as I can about you if you know what I mean? So I do not look like an oxymoron, smile, I feel I do seem like an oxymoron, to some people. Love you.

Ginette wrote: 17 Aug

Good morning my love,

I woke up today, and you're the first person on my mind, the thought of you brighten my day. I know it's all the doing of the Holy Spirit we have no control but to love each other according to the spirit that connects you and

I. How is my Zorro doing? Zorro is a cartoon I used to watch when I was a bit younger, in French. It's something that has the power to love and risk for others, so in my mind, a Zorro is a protector, and you're that person to me.

In case you didn't know what I consider as Zorro .

Well, I know things get busy but never busy for the one that I love, so I'll always make time for you. I'm glad that you understand me very well. I'll still put you on track. I also want the best for you the same way you want the best for me. Ah, you're the child I'm carrying? A big child then lol Lil Eugene .

Oh ok, thanks she's at the right-hand side of the Lord, it's such a sad story, but such is life. Will always be in my prayers: she must be a nice person. Sad what had happened to her in the past, I know it was hard on her, and it's something that can't be forgotten easily.

Ginette wrote: 20 August

Hi sweetheart,

It's nice to hear from you, and I so appreciate all your lovely messages. How was your day? I just got back from work and thought to send a short note to let you know that I got all your messages and been thinking about you. I'll try to wait and see.

Yes, I'm fine, only hoping to move out of this place to a room. We are arranging my Mom's travel soon to Europe, so there's so much pressure on me. I'll have to go down to Calgary soon and will let you know. I hope you're doing okay. Fasting is a lot of work, especially when you have to go without regular intakes like food and water. That's good because it is through this, we get out quick prayers answered. Know that I'm thinking about you, honey. So tired . Much love! Hugs and kisses.

Ginette wrote: 22 August

Hi, my love,

Sorry for the silence things have been so busy these few days, and it hasn't been easy even to type a message, you know I hate that without you hearing from me. So I know it wasn't going to get through. I'll understand my love and would never get angry with you: I know it's not intentional. It is within minutes. My mom wants me in Calgary this weekend, so I'll be traveling there Saturday. She's supposed to move soon. She wants me to go with her but I can't for now due to work. Please keep us in prayers, okay. You're a particular person in my heart and know you're a part of my family for now. Once again, sorry for my delay. Hugs and kisses 😘

Thomas wrote: 22 August

In the fertile soil of God's grace, a chapter in our life has been granted, God came into our lives and had given eternal friendship. We have been blessed with God's blessings at last.

We are two souls that have received Christianity, raised to a new level of trust and honesty, not ever to be lost. And friends are friends forever, if the Lord is Lord of them, and a friend will not say "never" eternal welcome will not end.

We will keep each other close as always, it won't even seem we've gone, cause our hearts and big and small ways, will keep the eternal love that holds us secure.

Thank you, God, for this eternal friendship that will never end, cause compassion, and love for this friend show that a lifetime is not too long to live as friends. With the faith and love of God's giving, spring from the compassion we know, we will pray the joy we live in, that God will always show.

With faith and love, the Lord has given, springing from the hope we know. We will pray the joy you live in, Is the strength that now You show. I'll keep you close as always, and it won't even seem you've gone. Because the friendship and love with compassion, we have shown were given through amazing grace that only the miracles of God known. Love Thomas.

Ginette wrote: 24 August

Hello honey,

I think she understands you better than the many people in your family. Sometimes it's just one or two-person that gets along well in a large family.

I can imagine where you find yourself presently, in the middle of a crisis that only God can intervene. I get your message of the spirit of Jezebel in many people: they focus on materials than the lives of others, so whatever they must do to have others out of the way they will. Though Jezebel succeeded in her manipulations in the presence of Ahab and the kingdom, she didn't last forever: that's the exciting part of the story.

So it's the same for whosoever that possesses the spirit of Jezebel. Prayers do work, and I'm glad you look to God for solutions, God always has ears to listen to our cry when we need Him. I'll continue to pray for you from my end, that this situation will get under control.

Well, yes, I did read part of the attachments you sent, and I'll read further: they are exciting, and I can learn from them. Can't complain, honey, even if life seems to be complicated. I must be strong and face it with the faith of our Lord like I said I'll be traveling to Calgary tomorrow morning to help my Mom arrange her travel.

She's supposed to be leaving anytime next week.

You're right: no one is supposed to control another if even God, whose the creator of the universe, gives free will to the things He created to live what about we take in place of God? The only thing one can do is accept each other as we are, agree, and disagree this way, the team becomes stronger.

That's what I admired about you and me: we disagree and agree and do not try to control and see how much we are going smoothly. Not many people can, me Thomas and Ginette, Anna lol it's because we let God take the lead That's what God wants from us, my love.

Fasting shouldn't be that long, and God understands even before we pray, He only wants us to acknowledge Him, and believe me. He's forever willing to grant our honest prayers, not necessarily long prayers or fasts. God knows you're a sincere heart after Him, and many people can attest to that, even me from afar.

I'm mostly concerned about your health, my love. Thanks for continuing to keep me in prayers and always showing that love for me. I so appreciate everything about you, honey. I look forward to hearing from you gain. My regards. Your endless love. Hugs and kisses .

Ginette wrote: 26 August

Hiya, sweet man!

I finally arrived home! So thankful for a safe trip! How are you doing? Hope that you're having a good day, mine is also great, especially seeing my Mom again! 😀 She'll be traveling this Tuesday, so please, I need your prayers. I have been helping her arrange her stuff for the voyage. I'm beginning to miss her already, lol. I talked about you with her, and she's glad you're such a nice person and a God-fearing person. She thanks you so much for loving me and having that concern for her as well.

I was reading your last messages, and I see you got an excellent passenger this gone time lol. I think there's a problem with alcoholism there in your area. Wow, the description of the lady you met on your way to the meeting. Debbie sounds like a scary movie lol good you were kind to her, you seem a people person there, and I too know you're. I think a lot of people like you there.

Well, I have no issues with the emails you send at all: they make me feel closer to you: the only reason why it takes me some time to write back is my schedule. I do not feel obligated at all what I think is the will power to write again to show how much I appreciate your compliments. Your concerns care and love when you keep updating me on how you're doing isn't bad at all.

I know we will be together soon. The way God is putting things in place all will happen. You know this trip that my Mom is going on will also bring relief to us, and she went overseas several times after my dad passed.

There are properties and other things that belong to him that my mom hasn't taken care of. My Dad has an old extended family member who is getting of age, and he's the only surviving family there in Malta. He has no children, so he's anxious about meeting my Mom to give her what is rightfully for us. That's why I told you that we also have family issues but not similar to what you have there. No fights, lol. I can't wait to kiss you, honey, my Mom would be proud of meeting you some days same as me too.

One thing I like you to know is that true love does not look at the odds: having each other is the most important thing to me. I don't look at the negative part of you, but think the best I can always love you. Don't ever think that I feel you're not capable of making me happy, you do, and I feel so glad. With all the beautiful things you write to me, I think excellent having you as a partner, a mentor, and a great friend. I will forever smile for our meeting and will show that love for you no matter what.

Know that you're the sweetest man that I know apart from God and my Dad. Enjoy your day, honey. You're my Zorro and my endless love. Hugs and kisses .

Ginette wrote: 28 August

Hey honey,

Sorry, it seems like I have ignored your messages but not so, nothing intentional, not at all: I just been occupied with arranging my mom's traveling and her taking off. She left this evening to Milan then to Valletta, Malta. It's 16 hours, 55 minutes plus travel. Please keep her in prayers.

My day was hectic, but it is worth it when I'm doing it for mom: she's my best friend! I'm beautiful, just anxious to know my mom arrives safely. I hope you're doing great as well, my love, know that you're always in my heart and prayers as well. And I so appreciate your prayers and concern for my mom and me.

I'm quite exhausted, so I'll write later, probably tomorrow. I will be leaving for Montreal Friday. I thought it's good you hear from me, so you know what is going on and that I'm doing fine.

Enjoy your night, my love. Sweet dreams! Your wife to be. Hugs and kisses .

Thomas wrote: 28 August

You must be exhausted, sweetheart, take your time getting back to me when the spirit moves you. You're not so busy, and God lets me know that you are doing fine. I had that spiritual feeling the only thing that you should get some rest whenever you can. I know you do, and you and your mother are always in my prayers.

Makes me laugh, and I have to make her laugh if you called her she would have 10 million questions for you, smile.

I have to pray extra hard to make sure I can provide for the family, and it will be God's will that I do. One thing I miss about not being able to help people. And my faith is unshakable, and God will provide, I just want you to feel safe and secure and know in your heart that I can take care of you and the children.

I pray that you understand what I am trying to say, I love you. I must let it go and if it's meant to be it will come back, right now this very moment everything is okay.

You must be exhausted going back and forth, and I wish I were there so I can give you a nice gentle back rub and neck rub, have you go to sleep and get some rest. I love you I miss you and will eternally be with you.

God bless with love and prayers, your husband, and, most importantly, my soulmate. Sweet, beautiful Ginette.

Let me know as soon as your mother gets to her destination safely. She will be exhausted as well when she gets there, and I am tired, so I am going to get some rest. Gorgeous, I love you.

Ginette wrote: 29 August

Hi honey

It's always great to hear from you, you make me smile each time with your sense of humor, you're a funny guy, and I like that. How is my mentor, my Prince Charming, doing today? I hope you're doing great and having a fun day. Mine is going great, and I'm glad that Mom arrived safely praise God!

Well, I got some quality rest and can think right now . Your prayers and love for us are always appreciated and know as well that our is still with you. They say the spirit is willing to please God, but the flesh is weak: that been said, my soul is always ready to write to this special man who is so understanding.

Well, my prayers are with you, and I always ask God to keep you alive longer. Some people are older than you that are still kicking, so I have that faith that you can even see our grandkids.

God has everything in His hands: we only have to believe like you have been doing. My love, there's a saying that goes, "Our delays are not our denial" the issue with the park may be slow, but it will surely be solved.

I understand your feeling about us and believe me, and I try to be following most of my life or to be like everyone. I try to work on my character each time. I so need your gentle rub honey because I missed being massaged. Going back will take much from me, and I'll surely be tired. I have no choice lol. It's always my pleasure hearing from you, honey. I look to hearing from you once again. Enjoy the rest of your day. My regards to you and hugs and kisses. Your wife.

Thomas wrote: 29 August

Smile I love you, sweetheart, I pray your day is going well, and I pray you are feeling well. Anyway, I just received a call from Vinnie Capone, and we will have known for about 25 years. If you're not familiar with the last name Capone, his uncle was Al Capone, a gangster in the Mafia out of Chicago Illinois, in the 30s 40s and 50s.

He had over 400 people killed, and he shot 40 himself, he was finally sent to San Quentin Prison in the San Francisco Bay Area.

Where he had syphilis, and the authorities let him live out the rest of his life in Florida where he died. Vinnie is alive and well, who calls me from, Arizona. Asked me if I would speak for him at a big meeting this coming Friday night.

Let me explain Vinnie Capone, a little background, being one of the best trumpet players in the world, and there was a time he traveled with Count Basie band. When he was in Florida, a couple of goons found out that he was a Caponi. I'm sure there are relatives of the poor unfortunate souls that his uncle Al Capone killed. They broke both of his legs, broke his ribs, shot him twice, beat him, and put him in a concussion were miraculously he woke up in a hospital.

The goons came back to the hospital to visit him, to break his heart. They said, "we are so sorry, Vinnie, we did not mean to do that," and then left. As a result, Vinnie Capone is not quite all there mentally and never will be. He talks nonstop, one gift that he did not lose was the ability to play his trumpet.

He plays for one of the most prominent Catholic churches in Arizona, where I have watched him play. He can play the piano and the trumpet at the same time, a very gifted musician.

I have also watched him play in a recording studio where he was playing his trumpet along with the Symphony lady who was playing the piano. They made recording together that I have somewhere, and I will try to find it and send it to you. The owner of the recording studio was selling the CDs before we even left the recording studio.

He is always broke and has to always Halk his trumpet to a pawnshop to get money to live. And whenever I used to go, I would have to give him the cash to get his trumpet out of Hawk. He just left a message on my telephone answering machine and wants methis Friday night and speak for him. He is the type of person you cannot stand to be around, and he never shuts up. And I understand that it is to his mental instability of what happened to him when those two goons in Florida tried to kill him.

Another interesting fact that I may have mentioned to you, not sure if I. have, would you happen to know who John Newton was? He was a captain of a ship. That transported African-American slaves from Africa to the United States and Europe, he was not a very nice man, as a matter fact, he was evil.

He found God and turn his life around. In doing so, he wrote one of the most beautiful songs of the world, "Amazing Grace."

He recalls listening to the slaves that were chained below in his ship. The moans they would hum harmoniously was the tune we now associate with the song, "Amazing Grace."

That tone on the piano can only be played on the. Black keys. I just heard that the other day while I was watching a ministry program on YouTube. I thought it was fascinating and miraculous.

One more exciting scenario, Thomas was visiting Ginette in Canada during a severe winter storm, it was a blizzard of biblical proportion, and no one was out. The owner of a donut shop was about ready to close his shop when in stumbled Thomas. There was frost in his hair: he was frostbitten, shivering, and ask the owner, "can I please have a sweet roll?" And the owner, in disbelief, that anyone would go out in the storm, said, "are you married?" And Thomas answered, "of course I'm married to my girl Ginette." You do not think my mother would send me out in this weather, do you?

A quadruple smile I love you, God bless with love and prayers. Your husband, who has finally thawed out. Quadruple smile LOL.

I love you, my beautiful sweet young Ginette.

SEPT 2018, ROMANTIC MEMOIRS FROM HEAVEN

Ginette wrote: 2 September

Good morning Honey, just a short note. I'm in a hurry out now, and I'll message more or call in the evening. I got all your messages — just a few pictures for you.

Ginette wrote: 4 September

Hello sweetheart,

It has been a few days since you heard from me. I have been in the hospital again for my knees since I got back to Montreal. I feel a bit better now, praise the Lord! How have you been keeping as well? I hope that you're blessed. I hate when I keep silence from you, but I had no choice because the pain becomes unbearable, and I don't think straight unless I take morphine.

I have read all your sweet messages, and believe me, and it feels great doing that. You're right, my love, and I too think our meeting is never perchance but something that was meant to be.

Before we were born the destiny was already set, God never makes a mistake because He knows now, later and tomorrow, we do not have the abilities to know such unless God is with us.

Having your child will be my very first experience, and I feel God has a reason why He wants to make you the first person to make me have a child. If it was meant for another guy, it was to be ever since I guess, but nothing happen perchance. I realize our meeting plus the month are inline, not our programming or timing, but God's timing even though we a had a little disagreement lol. God is stronger, you see.

You were asking about Mom, and she's doing great, there with one of my Uncle. He's the one helping her get around. I told her you to ask about her each time, and she said: C'est gentil de sa part! Guess you want to know the meaning lol. I won't know anything you look for the purpose: I want to test your French ability 😆 .

Do you ask if I agree to have your child? My answer is yes, of course! It is not just crucial for you but for me as well. Life isn't only short for you but us, so yes, I'm prepared to be a mother. I know you genuinely love me, it's one reason I have decided to go a long way with you. You're a good man Thomas! Getting sick made it all worse, but praise I'm fine now.

I look forward to hearing from you, my love. Enjoy your day — hugs and kisses 😘 from me.

Ginette wrote: 5 September

Hi sweetheart,

It's a pleasure getting your message as I wasn't sure my message went through yesterday. You're so kind to ask about how my mom and I are keeping. Mom is doing great, and I am now as well after a few days of pain. Well, the cause of the pain in my knees was the result of an accident

I had in the past. I had it during the very first experience to drive a car, and it was my Dad's car. I didn't know how to drive by then, and I had my knees hit below the steering. The pain goes and comes. Sometimes for months, I don't experience the pain. I don't take morphine all the time: it's only when the pain starts. The doctor told me the pain would stop: it's just a matter of time. Well, I'm okay now, and I so appreciate your prayers, my love. Thanks so much for the reminder that I'm your only love, so do you for me, honey. I have no one else on my mind for the future, but you.

It's a piece of great news that you were able to know the exact dates to meet the doctor. My prayers are for this to go as we wish, and with God, all things are possible. I think and pray about this every day, and I know what we want will come to past. God knows it all, so no need for us to worry that much. They understand what this means. I do the same for my Mom as well, and I do that to fulfill God's love.

Like I said the other time, the truth is just the truth they'll realize one day. I'll continue to pray for this situation.

Also, I'll look into it concerning what you ask about if there is a buyer I know, I have no idea yet, but I'll look into that. Have a great night, honey. I love you so much. Hugs and kisses 😙 .

Thomas wrote: 5 September

First of all, let me start by saying my prayers are with you and your mother, and of course, my love always for you. May I ask a question, please? And as your husband who cares for his wife and the mother of our children, what is going on with your knees?

Because I care and God loves you, and they found out why you are getting pain in your knees? And other than morphine to reside the pain, what can be done to cure your illness?

I know you realize that morphine is a very, very addictive drug. If that's the only drug they can use to cure your pain, you are in severe pain. And I am going too fast longer in prayer because you are all I think about, you're my only wife I will ever have. The only soulmate I will ever have on this earth as we know it.

You are my life and my wife for the rest of our life. Not only that, I not only care for my angel, but God also does as well, and so does your mother.

And no matter what, you will always be the only woman in my life

because you're my girl. Ever and forever on this earth as we know it and in heaven for eternity. I will never be in love with my precious angel with anyone or have I ever been in love with anyone as I have you.

God knows the answer to our prayers, and I am faith with works. Blessed with love and prayers to my sweet precious lovely Angel, whom I adore, and I love you with prayers. Hugs and kisses, your husband.

Ginette wrote: 7 September

Good morning my love,

Hope you're having a good day so far, mine is going great, I woke up not too long ago and about to leave for work.

Sorry I was not able to message you back as quickly as I wanted. I was so exhausted last night, as I was busy yesterday since I didn't go to work for a few days. I had to work more.

I think our relationship is going great because we two have our hearts together, and in the Lord. No connection or friendship can work when those involved refuse to understand. We have passed that stage and moving on: mind you, it wasn't smooth from the onset lol. We needed to disagree to agree.

Wow, what a great writer! You know I realize that as you wrote about the miracle, I keep following and understand how you placed those words neatly and each sentence needed in a miracle. I love that so much you're good at writing to admit.

Well, you're right, my love, no one knows about what we share inside, and it would be great to surprise everyone when I'm in my five months of pregnancy. People will be so amazed that you have not told them. Keep important things to us is good because our God even works in secret for us, at the end of it's for our good.

I look forward to hearing from you soon. My prayers are with you each day, and you enjoy the rest of your day — hugs and kisses 😘 *to my endless love.*

Ginette wrote: 9 September

Good morning sweetheart,

I hope you're having a great Sunday! Mine is going great and sweet I can relax. Things are always busy during the week, so Saturdays and Sundays are good days to relax. I wish I would go where I attend the community gathering, but it is far from here since I left Sophie's place.

My Dad's extended relative that I can refuse to as my Uncle is also called Samuel. He's the one doing the traveling with my Mom. What a coincidence in our lives! They are traveling soon, but Mom hasn't told me where I'd ask her.

Back to your nephew, I hate arguing so much, especially someone I love, you remember we did discuss from the onset as well? It stresses me very much. Not sure your nephew and his wife, who's the cause of the arguing there. Thanks, you were able to settle things between them. You're a good man Thomas.

Well, I wouldn't be happy if we get married and argue, better we make use of our marriage to be happy and take care of our children. We have already had our share of arguments, so I know we will be a better couple.

One thing I like you to understand is that having struggles with someone for tomorrow isn't a bad thing. I don't measure my love for someone base on materials, and it would make no sense to me to get involved with another guy, because of financial issues.

When I say, I love it is never a joke but something from within my heart.

I know things may not be too good, but I must understand. I know I'm free to do what I want but must also know that I'm involved with a man, and it's you. Understand?

It seems like the issue with your family inheritance is a huge problem, but it looks like the truth is unfolding. And it is when God is going to bring the enemies to shame. God is always great, and I know what you and your family's desires will surely come to the past. God never sleeps. Thanks once again for messaging me. Always great to hear from you. I'll do a few things and get some rest. Have a lovely Sunday, my love. And ✿ Your girl!

Ginette wrote: 11 September

Good morning my love,

No one believes what we believe, and they only see things from the surface and want to talk about the topic of the conversation you bring out to them.

Are they concern about what we have shared since we met?

The many messages we have share and the benefit of what we have? The happiness we have within our hearts, do they value these? Their concern is the money aspect, not what the young girl shares with this older man as she claims. Concerning me taking morphine for my pain doesn't mean that I'm hooked on it. I don't experience this each time only once in a while, so how is my child going to be a crack head? I can have other prescriptions when I have the pain I'm not an addicted person to morphine. I feel so insulted by your doctor friend.

Another thing I want you to understand is that I'm not saying you're the cause of all these been said: you have positive thoughts about me. But when this thing about meeting a young girl on the internet arises, all that get in the heads of these people are evil thoughts. Hence, then it's better people only make friends in their towns or communities, that's not possible they know these things, but instead of thinking both ways they prefer to be one-sided.

Do you think you're the only person having the fears? I do too, and I ask myself a lot of questions, I don't know what kind of person you're either if not from calls and emails. I think deeply because most war veterans have a hidden past and are involved in many things. Still, I prefer to leave this carnal thought and believe as a believer that whatever happens, it's God that allows, where is your faith, Thomas?

There you go! If you are honest, you know we do talk on the phone most of the time, it's just recently. I try my possible best to prove my love to you, but you keep taking everything back like I'm not showing love. So I give you an option, can you get involved with someone older than this young girl you will never understand?

I leave everything with you, and I look forward to your response. Have a good day. I'll always respect and love you no matter what distractions you have from people that don't know me but judge me so well. Enjoy your Sunday!

Thomas, 30 MAY

Ginette, did I mention to you that I want to marry you and that I love you. You are one in 1 million, my precious angel, and I'm going to love you. And we are going to love each other, that is God's will for us. I love you so much, and I think about you so much, I wish you were here. I love you, and I cannot stop loving you. I love you seriously, and you like those romance stories that I sent to you? I certainly enjoyed writing them to you, because I care you're worth, and God loves you.

Ginette, I know it's too late. I miss you. I want to be together with you so bad to mind those romantic stories I write to you? Seriously I do enjoy writing them to you. I will try to tone them down unless you want me to hit some high notes. Smile. You're the only honest lady I have ever met or talked to in 4 years. Can you believe that? Going to appreciate you so much and do everything I. can for you to make you happy. I do not want to smother you. I do not want to control you: I'm not jealous: it's a God-given gift that you and I even got together is the way I see It. And feel it spiritually.

I have a funeral to go to the 17ᵗʰ and then other funerals to go to June 10: all I'm going to send you the thing I made today. I forgot to send it. I love you.

How to nurture fruits of the spirit, you that you and I were meant to be? I have a spiritual feeling that nothing happens perchance, as a matter fact I know it does not it's God's plan and his will that would turn our will and life forward to not only ourselves, others around us,

Did I mention, I also feel spiritual that we are equally yoked. And that is my priority, always has been that you are the one for me and I will internally be the one for you.

I love to kiss you and with a French kiss for hours, not only hours but with our eternal life together. I know we have faith in God, loves us, and will take care of us provided for us. I already feel I have been blessed and an answer to my Prayer. A miracle we are going to write about, we are going to read a book together about what love is and should be between two people that love each other the way that we do. I love you so much,

Ginette, and I want to be with you so badly. Although years I have waited for you.

Let me know when you get the book sweetheart: God bless with love and prayers, your husband, Thomas. do not forget to say your prayers, very important and influential.

Do not forget to check your Yahoo email please sweetheart, I miss you, and I miss you and double down with love.

Ginette researching your middle name (Anna), can't understand why you do not like it? Although I found God's gift and a spiritual gift for your middle name. Very special, very precious, and only through the grace of God, working together, you will see how your middle name will manifest, the prophetic message that God would like you to give others.

God said to me: tell the people to repent, and I will heal their land. Tell them to repent? I questioned God, but they don't want to listen to me. They laugh at me, they mock me, and they scoff at me. And God Almighty said, "those who choose not to repent would die by the sword," and He showed me. A double edge sword. God gave me a vision about a war, that war is very near.

We need to warn people and encourage them to come to Christ. God, please help spread the word. All Christians need to be strengthened and know that God will take care of them as long as they stand firm and trust in our Savior, Jesus Christ, and God, our heavenly father.

To come to Christ, Love the people, hate the sin. Let's show people Jesus loves so that they can see the light we see. Let's not take part in things that are abominations to the holy God. Evil is why God will fill these prophecies, and I'm finally sending this out to everyone. Other Christians have had the same prophetic vision from God.

Unfortunately, many people will have doubts. Again, God has confirmed by revealing this same vision to multiple Christians who have never met or spoken to each other. Only people who don't know Christ knew how much God loves them and hate to see them die in these disasters. God loves us, and we need to repent so he can heal our land. Talk about it, the Lord said, some will listen, some won't, but the important thing is that everyone hears it and knows about it.

I pray that the Holy Spirit will touch your heart and guide you with this information: please pray and ask God for guidance and wisdom. I'm merely doing what God called me to do, and I'm just the messenger of the Lord, blessings to all, Ginette. This is your prophecy mission and spiritual gift in life, and this is the content of the name of your middle name. And you do know the context of your spiritual first name Ginette, which is why we are together.

The meaning of your name: is powerful and prophetic, as well as my first name, Thomas, "the twin." We are supposed to be together, robust, and reliable. With God and Jesus Christ on our side, we can save many souls together. You're worth it, and we love each other.

There is a reason God, through Jesus Christ, our Lord's name, joined us together.

I love you. I will always love you: we are soul mates that God has bonded together through Jesus Christ, our Lord's name. And, no matter what other people say or think, that you and I will both know in our hearts that we were meant to be together. God knows our fate and what will be revealed and our future together.

At your convenience, if you think it appropriate, I would be more than pleasantly pleased to call you on your phone. I would most certainly enjoy hearing your voice, enjoying one another's company and having fun together. I want to call you on your phone, only if it would be convenient. It is 3 p.m. right now, and I'll be waiting for you, sweetheart, a God-given gift of a treasured, through prayer.

And if it is God's will, and if it is God's will, we will have children together. If it's not, we have a lot of work to do for God to save souls, and the time is getting close

Observing the world situation and getting worse faster. Personally, Jesus Christ, our Lord, and whose second return will be soon. Still, I have not felt this, and God will come like a thief in the night we know not when. Jesus Christ, our Lord, came the first time as a lamb: Jesus Christ's second coming will be as a roaring lion.

I love how you love me, and God loves us both: first, I asked God why? Then as time passed and we got to know one another, I accepted that we were meant for one another with the grace of God. I will wait as long as I can to chat with you. I would certainly enjoy hearing from you. And if you let me know what a good time to contact you, I would be more than happy to: I care you're worth it. God loves you.

And I have work to do for God: we are to save many souls and unite together: we can do it together. To keep those lost souls, we can reach more people through our ministry. I am a minister, and we are all ministers. I love God and love preaching his word, and with you, with me, there's nothing we cannot do together.

No matter, you and I have work to do for God through Jesus Christ's name and the Holy Spirit working through us.

I love you. I realize you are busy. I do not feel sorry for anything in this first communicating: I understand, okay? I love you so much. I think about you continuously. You're always on my mind, and I want to tell people about this love we have found through our faith.

And with our faith, God willing, we will have children, and we will love one another romantically, with ecstasy, the passionate love others will covet, dream, and pray. With

God consensually bonding our love through holy grace, I would love you, respect you with compassionate kindness and care.

After I asked Diane for my girl's hand in holy matrimony, something to look forward to, on our honeymoon evening.

Gorgeous, you are my French vanilla flaming soufflé with a little French vanilla banana split ice cream, a little bit of crêpe Suzette, slowly pouring warm French raspberry syrup sparingly of course, with a bit of French chocolate syrup warm, I might also add sparingly, just a smidgen of French vanilla whipping cream, with a tasty little cherry on top, very pleasing to the palate, if I may be so kind to say so, sumptuous, luscious, delicious, mouthwatering, and removing is very patiently, and slowly, with Honorable intentions, and we give great compliments to the MasterChef, God Almighty. Thank you, God, with the lovingkindness, and being prayerful, with our unshakable faith, and our love for one another, this is what we look forward to at the appropriate time, very patiently, consensual, maybe three years down the road, possibly longer, smile,

Ginette, please do not feel sad or sorry for not connecting: it will happen in God's time, not ours. If you feel comfortable and are not nervous, I would love you to call me on my landline telephone. With visionary, prophetic love, Thomas

Thomas is going to love Ginette, like Ginette loves to be loved

Thomas and Ginette. More shall be revealed through the Grace of God, and this romantic interlude has only just begun. And with every passing moment picking up superhuman speed, that could have only come from God, our Father, in the precious blood of Jesus Christ, our Lord, witnessed through the Holy Spirit. Thomas would like to ask Ginette a question pertaining to raising a family and having children. Thomas finally meets Ginette at the airport?

THOMAS AND GINETTE SEND A CHRISTIAN DREAM LOVE LETTER, OF THEIR EXPECTATIONS.

Thomas's expectations:

Ginette made arrangements to fly to Arizona and stay with Thomas for a week. Tonight Ginette had boarded a plane in, Canada, and flew to, Arizona. Thomas was waiting with his friend, the limousine driver, Frank. It was everything they had expected with everything they have in common that did not happen perchance their meeting, preordained and as perfect as placing your hand in a glove. Thomas and Ginette just held each other at the airport, and God's love flowed through the Holy Spirit between the two of them.

Arriving at Thomas's home, that far exceeded Ginette's expectations. Thomas showed Ginette her new home: after some time, I should say a short time, they both had taken showers and separate showers. I came back to the master bedroom dressed and felt refreshed. Instantly they both just wanted to lay on the master bed and hold each other.

Thomas was going to show Ginette the sites taking her out to dinner. Ginette did not want to see any sites other than out of the windows of the home. Thomas provided the best foods and stocked the home. Thomas had a feeling, and Ginette reconfirmed that feeling by stating, "please let us not do anything other than spend the short time we have together: I want to be held, and I want you to keep me and let us look into each other's souls. They held one another for a long time, and this communicated and enjoyed each other's company. It was a spiritual connection so strong. Most of the time Ginette spent in Arizona with Thomas was like heaven on earth for both of them.

Although they found it very difficult not to fornicate. The secret to not having sex before marriage is continuous dating and communication between one another. Kissing on the lips was a polite form of fornication that they both knew was not the right time. Kissing on the lips and French kissing of the soft, moist lips would leave their minds uncontrollably to the feeling of lusting. The passion in the romantic moments was surreal and supernatural. God's love flowing between these two precious souls that came together through God's grace was so erotic and romantic.

They did not want to eat: they did not want to do anything but stay in each other's arms and hold each other and speak softly to one another. Thomas just loved Ginette's accent, and the beautiful French Canadian accent matched a beautiful heart and matched the drop dead gorgeous lady. God had undoubtedly sent one of his precious Guardian Angels into this Marine's life through prayer, faith, and love for one another and God. Very difficult to write the words I can even describe this type of love or even experience this love.

Ginette and Thomas are more than in love, and they are lovesick: they are not sick of love: they are both heartbroken when leaving the airport to separate. Separation is not in the eyes of these two children of God, and they're feeling the pain of separation. This love is precious, and all the gold in the world and the world as a whole could not even come close to this love.

Thomas and Ginette, their hearts are hurting: they do not want to leave each other's arms or lives after constant companionship, conversation, and communication. Although they both know that the communications have stopped between them, and the feelings surpass the communications. Words on paper words cannot describe the supernatural spiritual sense that the Holy Spirit working through both of them, of a love not known to them, or in their minds could ever be explained.

Thomas let Ginette know, keep in mind you are an orphan, and your mother, Diane, is a widow, needs to be cared for, and we will be back together shortly. Our communications will not cease: the only thing Thomas is feeling is the manly desire to go with Ginette on her journey with her mother. To Calgary, on to Montréal, and then to Malta. Thomas cannot even imagine living without Ginette. Thomas is finding it very difficult to get back to somewhat of life without Ginette.

Although God's will and a great calling through the Holy Spirit for these two precious souls. They find themselves jumping back into the fire to refine the gold, what God has joined together, let no man put asunder. The trials and tribulations are why so-called bad things happen to good people because God loves these precious souls. Thomas and Ginette know this and have to suffer the anxiety of separation.

Like Jesus Christ our Lord in a tiny aspect, he separated from his father God and the people separated from Jesus Christ, the most precious love of the soul. Some souls are blinded and will never know, and some eyes will be opened, and they will know the love in their journey has an eternal life of love with God in heaven.

They hugged each other had their rooms lie down on the bed for hours, looking into each other's souls. You could feel the love that flowed through the Holy Spirit in between these two precious souls. God has a calling for them that far surpasses their understanding.

Ginette's expectations: My experience and Expectations of Arizona. After the twist and turn of life in 3 years, meeting the love of my life at the airport was the greatest joy and miracle that happen to me. Seeing the smiles on our faces and tears rolling down our eyes shows how much love we have for each other. The greatest surprise is my husband Thomas renting a limousine to pick me up and the driver being his friend having the patience to wait his entire day at the airport with my husband for my arrival.

As we drove from the airport and approached, the people wondered where the limousine was headed. We noticed the same surprise on the faces of people along the way: as we get closer to the quiet town which my husband refers to as God's country, people could not take their eyes off the limousine, some people drove the direction of the limousine to be sure where exactly this was headed, which area or house, I saw a lovely looking house from a distance and my husband whispered in my ears that this is your house my gorgeous, beautiful, delicious sweet lady!

I couldn't believe that we were actually in the town and near the house: I could see people distance away, watching closely to see who is going to get down from the limousine: the driver got down first and opened the door for me, and as I got down the driver was busy unloading my suitcases while I helped my husband Thomas to get down and entered our house, I knew in my heart this was going to be the talk of the town.

We got back out from the house to see the limousine driver take off, and he said Thomas take care and contact me anytime! Also, take good care of this beautiful angel! And we all smile. We then went back into the house, and Thomas asked me what I wanted for a drink before taking a shower. I said just water very cold, and I was served with the water.

For a minute or two, Thomas said, beautiful, let me show you your room and that of your mother and the bathroom, and after you are done with your shower, I'll show you the dungeon or maybe tomorrow. I was so excited as he shows me around, and I could see how decent and neat the house was: Thomas shows me the boxes that would be open at a later-day, and believe me, I knew I have a lot of work waiting for me, lol.

As we got into the master bedroom, I noticed the bedding wasn't well arranged, and Thomas said, oh my gosh! I didn't think you were coming today, and I slept in your bed last night and believed me I felt I did arrange your bed neatly, and we laughed about it and said to him that doesn't let me tie you up the very first day! We were laughing so hard.

I then went to get my shower and change my clothes: in the process of doing that, I got dressed and made my way to the living room, Thomas appears from the kitchen, and I said I was just about to call you out loud to know where you were. Thomas said I was in the kitchen, he hastily went back in the kitchen and before I know it he already made a hot meal, and I was so surprised how fast he was, and I was served and asked him can we eat?

He said sure, but not together lol I knew he was shy, or he just wanted me to be free and enjoy my meal. I got done with my meal, and I couldn't believe that a man-made such a delicious meal! After I got done with eating and him as well, we went back in the living room, sitting opposite each other and looking at each other with smiles, none of us were ready to start a conversation, and I said, hey Thomas, you didn't ask about the girls and

Thomas said oh my! I knew from the airport we were so delighted and emotional and didn't talk much and he said I forgive my careless attitude. I was so thrilled, and I said sure me too, and he said, how are our mother and the rest of the family and friends keeping?

I said everyone is doing very great! Then Thomas said, let's give Diane a call to let her know that you arrived safely and that you're right here with me. We call, and my mother was so excited and spoke French over the phone, asking me about the trip and what I think about Thomas so far? I said, mom Thomas is a very great person, but I still look forward to giving you the report because it's just the first day.

As it approaches the evening hour, Thomas then made dinner for us, and as we were done, he chatted for so many hours till midnight, and he said, beautiful, go and get some rest to pray before you sleep, and I told you too, and we said good night to each other. The next morning Thomas was awake at 6 am,

waiting till I was up, I then woke up at 7 am, and breakfast was ready, and we had breakfast, and he said can you drive? I said, not at all have you forgotten?

He said I was kidding you. I know you don't, and his Marine friend was with the car, and he said, hey, I need you right away! His friend was home in about 20 minutes, and he said, this is Ginette, my wife: she's from Canada and speaks French, and he said that was great! Welcome to Arizona! I said yes, for sure I woke up with the sunlight, and we all laughed about it. He volunteers to drive us to the stores to purchase what we needed when I'll be there: we left and got back home. I asked Thomas what he needed, and Thomas said poutine for sure I said, you know there's nothing we purchased that can make poutine, I told you the silly man you want to buck me right lol I made an American dish of which Thomas helped coach me to prepare, I made us a cheese burger, and we had that.

Thomas took me to some of the best places, and we had much fun: my whole stay very remarkable, something I'll never forget about. We slept in different rooms my entire stay for the month, not indulging in any fornication: we work on our books and arrange our house. Living with Thomas for a month was the most incredible experience I had, and I realize Arizona has so much potential: I fell in love with the weather, the food, and people I met, it changed my perceptions about Arizona because all along I thought it was all about crimes and immoral things. The countryside of Arizona is like heaven. When my husband Thomas told me it was God's country, I didn't believe but honestly, it is God's country—looking forward to moving back there to live permanently with Thomas and taking my mother with me.

Time-Spokes Through A Keyhole

And more shall be revealed.

We will always be friends: keep that in mind no matter what, we have spent quality time getting to know one another. I will pray for you because I care, and prayer is powerful: that is the faith with works. Have a good night, and it will be God's will, do not forget to say your prayers, sweet dreams: nothing happens perchance: we are both tired. Thank you, God, for my friend.

MEMOIRS OF ROMANCE, EXCITEMENT AND MIRACLES

To Be Continued…

Printed in the United States
By Bookmasters